INTRODUCTION TO
JEWISH LAW OF THE SECOND
COMMONWEALTH

INSTITUTUM IUDAICUM, TÜBINGEN

OTTO MICHEL und MARTIN HENGEL

ARBEITEN ZUR GESCHICHTE DES ANTIKEN JUDENTUMS UND DES URCHRISTENTUMS

BAND XI

INTRODUCTION TO JEWISH LAW OF THE SECOND COMMONWEALTH

PART 1

LEIDEN

E. J. BRILL

1972

INTRODUCTION TO JEWISH LAW OF THE SECOND COMMONWEALTH

BY

ZE'EV W. FALK

PART 1

LEIDEN
E. J. BRILL
1972

ISBN 90 04 035 370

CONTENTS

PREFACE

This book is an attempt to describe Jewish Law in actual operation in the days of the Second Temple. This was the period when laws developed which were later restated in Tannaitic literature, and when laws were put to the test of political life and not only to that of reasonings of the academies. In this way I hope to prove "the historical unity and uninterrupted development of Jewish Law " from the time when Scripture was determined until the Oral Law was edited in the Midrash and the Mishna.

Indeed I have frequently been obliged to depend on speculation and on comparisons with the development of other legal systems, and I admit that the contents of this book amount only to one interpretation, which often deviates from the approach of our Sages, and perhaps even from the logical reason of the reader. There certainly are other methods to reconcile the contradictions between the sources referred to, not as distinct stages of a general development, but as expressions of differences of opinion among the sages. My purpose is not to determine the halakha itself but to propose an introduction to it, and every reader may seek his own means of entering its halls.

It would have been proper to attend in detail to the writings of both the ancient and latter-day scholars of Israel, and especially those of my teachers Professors J.N. Epstein, H. Albeck, A. Alon and S. Assaf, of blessed memory, and Professor I. Baer, may he be spared for long life. I would thus have most certainly found many places where I differed from them or where I found myself in agreement with them. But for the sake of my pupils I could no longer delay publication of the book; "who can discern errors ?".

For a similar reason I was content to use translations when quoting from the Apocrypha (following Cahana's edition, except for Ecclesiasticus and Judith, for which I used Segal's and Grinz' books), from Philo and from Josephus (I have used the Loeb Classical Library and translations by Shalit and Simhoni). Anyone wishing to stress the research of these sources may consult them in the original, and my purpose was merely to refer the reader to them. The Judean Desert scrolls are quoted according to the Haberman edition, the Mishna according to the Yalon-Albeck edition and in the second volume according to the Kaufmann and Cambridge manuscripts, the Tosephta

according to Lieberman and from the middle of Nashim- according
to Zuckermandel.

This is the contents of lectures I have been delivering during the
past five years in the Tel-Aviv University, at the initiative of the
late Professor Benjamin de Vries. I wish to acknowledge the kindness
of Rabbi S. Meron, who made numerous comments, Professor Dr.
Otto Michel, who accepted this book into the series of publications
under his editorship, and Mr. E.N. Dembitz who translated the text
from Hebrew.

May this book draw threads of grace and of good favour from the
words of the Scribes and the Elders unto those who devote themselves
to Torah and to public affairs in the home of our life.

Jerusalem   Z.W. Falk

ABBREVIATIONS

Albeck, Introduction	H. Albeck, Introduction to the Mishna (Hebrew) Jerusalem-Tel Aviv 1959
Albeck, Mishna	H. Albeck, The Mishna, with introductions, commentary and addenda, (Hebrew) Jerusalem-Tel Aviv 1953-59
Alon, History	G. Alon, History of the Jews in Palestine in the Time of Mishna and Talmud (Hebrew), Tel Aviv 1953
Alon, Studies	G. Alon, Studies in Jewish History in the 2nd commonwealth and the time of Mishna and Talmud (Hebrew), Tel Aviv 1957
AP	Aramaic Papyri
BA	Biblical Archeologist
BASOR	Bulletin of the American Schools of Oriental Research
Belkin, Philo	S. Belkin, Philo and the Oral Law (Harvard Semitic Series, 11) Cambridge, Mass. 1940
Bickerman, Inst.	E. Bickerman, Institutions des Séleucides, Paris 1938
BZ	Biblische Zeitschrift
BZAW	Beihefte zur ZAW
CBQ	Catholic Biblical Quarterly
Cohen, JRL	B. Cohen, Jewish and Roman Law, New York 1966
Cowley, AP	A. Cowley, AP of the Fifth Century BC., Oxford 1923
CPJ	V.A. Tcherikover - A. Fuks - M. Stern, Corpus Papyrorum Judaicarum, Cambridge, Mass. 1957-64
Deut	Deuteronomy
de Vries, History	B. de Vries, Studies in the Development of the Talmudic Halaka[2] (Hebrew), Tel Aviv 1966
de Vries, Introd.	B. de Vries, Introduction to Talmud and Halakha (Hebrew), Tel Aviv 1965
DJD	P. Benoit - J.T. Milik - R. de Vaux, Les grottes de Murabba'at, Discoveries in the Judaean Desert II, Oxford 1961
Epstein, Ta. Lit.	J.N. Epstein, Prolegomena ad litteras tannaiticas (Hebrew), Jerusalem 1957
Ex	Exodus
Finkelstein, Pharisees	L. Finkelstein, The Pharisees[3], Philadelphia 1962
Falk, HL	Z.W. Falk, Hebrew Law in Biblical Times, Jerusalem 1964
Falk, JML	Z.W. Falk, Jewish Matrimonial Law in the Middle Ages (Scripta Judaica, 6), London 1966
Gulak, Obligation	A. Gulak, History of Jewish Law. Talmudic Period, Law of Obligation and its Guaranties (Hebrew), Jerusalem 1939
Gulak, Urkundenwesen	A. Gulak, Das Urkundenwesen im Talmud, Jerusalem 1935
Hönig, Sanh.	S. Hoenig, The Great Sanhedrin, Philadelphia 1953 (cited according to Hebrew ed., Jerusalem 1961)
HTR	Harvard Theological Review
HUCA	Hebrew Union College Annual

IEJ	Israel Exploration Journal
JBL	Journal of Biblical Literature
JJP	Journal of Juristic Papyrology
JJS	Journal of Jewish Studies
Jones, Cities	A.H.M. Jones, The Cities of the Eastern Roman Provinces, Oxford 1937
Jones, Law	J.W. Jones, The Law and Legal Theory of the Greeks, Oxford 1956
JQR	Jewish Quarterly Review
JSS	Journal of Semitic Studies
Kaser, RPR	M. Kaser, Das römische Privatrecht (Handbuch der Altertumswissenschaft X.III.3) München 1955-59
Kaser, RZPR	M. Kaser, Das römische Zivilprozessrecht (Handbuch der Altertumswissenschaft X.III.4) München 1966
Kraeling, AP	E.G. Kraeling, The Brooklyn Museum AP. New Haven 1953
Lev	Leviticus
Lieberman, Greek	S. Lieberman, Greek in Jewish Palestine, New York 1942
Lieberman, Hellenism	S. Lieberman, Hellenism in Jewish Palestine, New York 1950
Lieberman, Tos. Kif.	S. Lieberman, Tosefta Kifshutah (Hebrew), New York 1955 ff.
Lipsius	J.H. Lipsius, Das attische Recht und Rechtsverfahren, Leipzig 1905-15
M	Mishna
Mantel, Sanh.	A. Mantel, Studies in the History of the Sanhedrin (Harvard Semitic Series, 18) Cambridge, Mass. 1961
MB	Münchener Beiträge zur Papyrusforschung und antiken Rechtsgeschichte
MGWJ	Monatschrift für die Geschichte und Wissenschaft des Judentums.
Neh	Nehemia
NTSt	New Testament Studies
Num	Numeri
PEQ	Palestine Exploration Quarterly
Rabin, QS	Ch. Rabin, Qumran Studies (Scripta Judaica, 2), London 1957
RB	Revue Biblique
RE	Pauly-Wissowa, Realencyclopädie der klassischen Altertumswissenschaft, 1892 ff.
RIDA	Revue internationale des droits de l'antiquité
Schalit, Herod	A. Schalit, König Herodes (Studia Judaica, 4) 1969 (cited from the Hebrew edition, Jerusalem, 1960)
Seidl, PtRG	E. Seidl, Ptolemäische Rechtsgeschichte² (Ägyptologische Forschungen, 22) Glückstadt 1962
T	Tosefta
Taubenschlag, Law	R. Taubenschlag, The Law of Greco-Roman Egypt in the Light of the Papyri, New York 1944
TB	Babylonian Talmud
Tcherikover, Hellenistic	V.Tcherikover, Hellenistic Civilization and the Jews, Philadelphia 1959
TJ	Palestinian Talmud

TRG	Tijdschrift voor Rechtsgeschiedenis
Tchernowitz, History	Ch. Tchernowitz, History of the Oral Law (Hebrew) New York 1934-50
VT	Vetus Testamentum
Weiss, GPR	E. Weiss, Griechisches Privatrecht auf rechtsvergleichender Grundlage, Leipzig 1923
Wolff, Beiträge	H.J. Wolff, Beiträge zur Rechtsgeschichte Altgriechenlands und des hellenistisch-römischen Ägypten, Weimar 1961
Wolff, Justizwesen	H.J. Wolff, Das Justizwesen der Ptolemäer (MB, 44) München 1962
Yaron, Introduction	R. Yaron, Introduction to the Law of the Aramaic Papyri, Oxford 1961
ZAW	Zeitschrift für die alttestamentliche Wissenschaft
ZSS	Zeitschrift der Savigny Stiftung für Rechtsgeschichte
Zucker, Studien	H. Zucker, Studien zur jüdischen Selbstverwaltung im Altertum, Berlin 1936

HISTORY OF THE SECOND COMMONWEALTH
AND HISTORICAL SOURCES

The days of the Second Temple comprise five periods of domination of the country. In the first period (538-333 B.C.E.) the exiles were privileged to settle in Judea, to erect the temple and to maintain autonomy according to the Law of the Torah within the framework of the Persian empire. After the country was conquered by Alexander the Great there began the period of Hellenist rule (333-166), which in turn is divisible into Alexander's rule (333-323) and the various periods of the Ptolemaids and the Seleucids which followed. Following the rebellion there began the third period, that of the Hasmonean dynasty (165-37), at the end of which Judea was drawn into the Roman empire. The rule of Herod, king by the grace of the Romans, opened the fourth period (37 B.C.E.-66 C.E.), and was followed by more or less direct rule of the Romans. The days of the Second Temple close with the short period of the rebellion (66-70), when there was again Jewish autonomy in the country, only to come to an end with the Destruction.

The history of Jewish law in the days of the Second Temple closely follows the various periods of political history, for the operation and development of law depend on the attitude of the rulers towards it. Regarding the Persian period we have no direct information other than of the liberal attitude of the authorities. If we would rather not avail ourselves of the assumption of biblical criticism, we may draw conclusions regarding the legal system that obtained at the time from those parts only of Scripture, that describe the period explicitly, and, further, from certain books of the Apocrypha,[1] from documents of the Jewish military colony in Upper Egypt,[2] and from Aramaic documents from Samaria.[3] We must also pay attention to the archives of the house of Murashu,[4] which refer to many transactions under

---

[1] E.g., the Book of Tobias and the Book of Judith, see J.M. Grinz, inH. Albeck Jubilee Book (Hebrew), Jerusalem 1963, pp. 123-151.

[2] See R. Yaron, Introduction, and JJS XII (1961), pp. 165-168.

[3] A. Rainey, PEQ IC (1967) 32-41; F.M. Cross, BA XXVI (1963) 110-121, HTR LIX (1966) 202-211.

[4] See Tarbiz (Hebrew) XXXVII (1967/8), 39-47; G. Cardascia, Les archives des Murashu, Paris, 1951.

Neo-Babylonian law to which Jews were parties. The usages of the
Samaritans and the version of the Pentateuch which they preserve
are also relevant in investigating the period, as resemblances between
them and the Halakha testify to a common tradition having existed
in the times when relationships between Jews and Samaritans were
still normal. We shall however have to depend mainly as far as the
earliest part of the period is concerned, on traditions of later date, and
it will not be easy to decide if there is anything reliable to depend on.
Certain conclusions may be arrived at, regarding the more ancient
Halakha, by examining it at later stages and by comparing it to other
legal systems. Although we shall be drawing on assumptions rather
than on sources, it is only proper that we make the attempt, in order
to cast some light on this important period which has been keeping in
the shade and in order to draw up some general hypotheses, which may
be subjected to critical examination later on as more source material
becomes available.[1]

Far richer is our knowledge of Jewish Law during the Hellenistic
period. Some of the books of the Apocrypha, written in that period,
speak of law and administration, some conclusions may be drawn from
the interpretations of the Septuagint; and a number of Greek papyri
describe various transactions in which Jews took part. To the Hellenistic
period there should be ascribed the penetration of many Greek terms
into the Halakha, terms of instructive value in regard to the shape of
ancient law.[2] Besides these terms there is a remarkable similarity of
content to Greek pattern.[3] Even the dispute between the Sadducees and
the Pharisees, although belonging to the subsequent period, is at times
instructive regarding the Halakha in the days of the Hellenists.[4]

From this point onward we are in possession of direct traditions
handed down to us in Talmudic literature, in the Apocrypha and in
the writings of Philo of Alexandia[5] and of Josephus.[6] This is the,
period in which most of the institutes of Talmudic law were developed
afterwards to be set forth in the Midrashim and in the Mishna. In the
vicinity of the Dead Sea literary items from the period of the Destruction
are constantly being discovered, including bills in Hebrew, Aramaic and

---

[1] See J. Pirenne. RIDA[3] I (1954) 195-217.

[2] Lieberman, Greek; id., Hellenism.

[3] I. Baer, Zion (Hebrew) XVII (1951/2) 1-65, XXVII (1961/2), 117-155.

[4] See p. 8 ff.

[5] Belkin, Philo.

[6] See literature in A. Schalit's translation of Josephus' Antiquities (Hebrew), Jerusalem
Tel Aviv, 1944

Greek,[1] and thus furnishing a certain perspective to the information in Halakha literature.[2] The Gospels also contain various legal details complementary to the information we have from Talmudic sources.[3]

The main difficulty lies, of course, in dating the various norms, especially where we have to rely on the Mishna, which was finally edited as late as 200 C.E. However, even the late Mishna often reflects earlier phases of the legal developments. As already pointed out by Zecharia Frankel in his Introduction to the Mishna, Leipzig 1859, archaisms in style (e.g. M Baba Kama I 2) may be taken as an indication of an early date. Where the sages discuss the interpretation of a certain rule, that rule must have been in existence before their time (e.g. M Qiddushin I 1). Likewise, where a reform was introduced, we may conclude what was the law prior to that reform (e.g. T Kethuboth XII 1). We should, moreover, analyse the complex halakha of the later period in order to find the simple elements preceding it. In accordance with the programmatic paper of Professor I. Baer on the Historical Foundations of the Halakha, we have to understand the various norms against their historical background, and may use the result for their dating.

The attempt made in this book seems to be complementary to the current literary and philological school of halakha. Jewish law cannot be understood without Jewish history, and its classical formulations were created much prior to their final, literary fixation.

Such a *legal archaeology* of halakha should also make use of stylistic indications, of names and *realia* and anything which is due to a specific historical situation. In addition we have always a *terminus a quo* for any given halakha, *viz.* the corresponding rule in biblical law, and a *terminus ad quem*, viz. the meaning accorded to it by a certain sage. Meanwhile a development must have taken place and it stands to reason that is has left its imprints even in the late sources,

---

[1] As of the present, the documents have been published in DJD II (1961) and J.T. Milik has also published two documents in Biblica XXXVIII (1957). Concerning the documents found in Israel, details were given in the Archaeological Survey of the Judaean Desert 1961, Journal of the Palestine Exploration Society (Hebrew) XXVI, 1962; see also J.T. Milik, VT Suppl. IV, 21.

[2] See e.g. Rabin, QS; Ch. Burchard, Bibliographie zu den Handschriften vom Toten Meer, BZAW 76 (1957), 89 (1965); Sanders, JBL LXXXVI (1967) 431-440; E. Koffmann, Die Doppelurkunden aus der Wüste Juda, Leiden 1968.

[3] Research of the Halakha in this literature has been done for some years past by J.D.M. Derrett. Cf. Nörr, ZSS LXXVII (1961) Rom. Abt. 92-141; Nörr, The Irish Jurist I (1966) 328-340; Steinwenter, JJP XV (1965) 1-19, and the vast literature on the trial of Jesus.

CHAPTER ONE

GROWTH OF THE HALAKHA

1. WRITTEN LAW

The Mosaic law was re-accepted on the Babylonian exile as binding law, and the group that returned from the exile based their regime on it : "For Ezra had set his heart to seek the law of the Lord, and to do it, and to teach in Israel statutes and ordinances" (Ezra VII 10). There were thus two things that engaged him : *to seek*, to expound the law for himself, and *to do it and teach it* to the others. This teaching refers of course to religion but it no doubt included the precepts of law and adjudication as well. Besides the study required in the process of settling disputes, it was also customary to read the Torah on various occasions, in the fashion described in Neh VIII 8 : "And they read in the book, in the Law of God, distinctly : and they gave the sense, and caused them to understand the reading". Reading the Torah included interpretation and Aramaic translation (TB Megilla 3a);[1] and in order to spread knowledge of the Torah and make it readable, Ezra went so far as to sanctify the books written in Aramaic (Assyrian) script, and perhaps even the translation into Aramaic (TB Sanhedrin 21b).[2]

Among the important laws which were expounded on the basis of the Torah was the commandment regarding the Feast of Tabernacles (Neh VIII. 14), but it may be assumed that in the course of public reading many matters were revived. The feeling was thus implanted in the people that they must alter their ways, and that among other things they must put away their foreign wives, "and let it be done according to the law" (Ezra X 3). Indeed, in this matter already they extended the purview of the Torah to include laws expounded by Ezra and not contained in the Torah proper, for the original prohibition

---

[1] See Segal, Introduction to the Bible (Hebrew), Jerusalem, 1952, 830. As to reading of the Torah see Tractate Soferim 10.

[2] Segal, Introduction, 848; J. Mann, The Bible as Read and Preached in the Old Synagogue, Cincinnati, 1940-1966.

referred to the seven nations only who lived in the land of Canaan
during the days of Moses.[1]

There were certain commandments which were not observed, the
written provisions of the Torah notwithstanding, and reasons for
this were apparently given at an early period. A case in point is the
rule concerning the "daughter that possesseth an inheritance", requiring her to marry within her tribe (Num XXXVI 8). The author
of the book of Tobias held that this requirement was still in effect,[2]
whereas the Scribes and the Sages considered it void, maintaining
that it existed in the generation of the wilderness but no longer obtained
(TB Baba Bathra 120a).

Laws derived from an explicit pentateuchal source are *words of
Torah*, as distinct from *words of the Scribes*;[3] according to a later
formula there is a distinction between *a matter to which the Sadducees
agree* (TB Sanhedrin 33b, Horayoth 4a) and a matter to which they do
do not.

Words of Torah are ascribed to God, who gave them on Sinai for
all the generations, and they are considered the political law of the
community of the dispersion. Hence the Septuagint came to translate
the word *Torah-nomos;* suggesting that the Torah is the law of the
Jews, with a standing comparable to the laws of the Greek *polis*. Due to
its divine source it is an accepted rule that the Torah is perfect and
nothing in it may be altered (Deut IV 2; XIII 1).[4] The exclusiveness
of the words of the written Torah was maintained chiefly among the
Sadducees, whereas the Pharisees nevertheless recognized new creations, as we will show later on.[5] And it is possible that the Pharisees
attributed the right to expound the Torah to the Sages alone, whereas
the Sadducees gave this right to everyone : "The Torah is bound up
and laid down, and anyone who wishes to may come and learn" (TB
Qiddushin 66a)[6].

---

[1] See TJ Qiddushin III 14, 64d; TB Aboda Zara 36b; Belkin, Philo, 233.

[2] And, apparently because of the dispute regarding the application of this law, went
so far as to say that an offender against it deserves the death penalty.

[3] Cf. Cohen, JRL, 277, 776.

[4] See Cohen, Law and Tradition, New York 1959, 4 f.

[5] As to the Sadducees see p. 10.

[6] Cf. the saying of Anan the Karaite : "Seek well in the Torah and depend not on my
opinion", which is perhaps a continuation of Sadducee doctrine. The words "in a corner"
in the present text giving the saying of the Sadducees were apparently added by the
Pharisees, so as to emphasize immediately the anticipated result, but cannot be assumed
to have been included in the saying of the Sadducees.

2. INTERPRATATION

Interpretation of the Torah was vested in Ezra and his fellow-Levites "that taught the people" (Neh VIII 9) : it was they who expounded and interpreted the scriptures. Their sayings are called *words of the Scribes;* they were read out together with the translation whenever the Torah was read in public. These explanations were preserved in the legal *Midrash* collections (such as Mekhilta, Sifra and Sifre) and in the Talmud, and also in the Septuagint, the Samaritan Pentateuch, the Aramaic translation (*Targum*) and in the writings of Philo and Josephus.[1]

Until the times of Shma'ya and Abtalion (40 B.C.E.) these latter-day interpretations were not considered reliable in the schools and evidence in their support was generally required to be brought from either the Scriptures or from a statute or a case in point. The increasing expansion of the system of *Midrash* came to be one point of dissension between the Pharisees and the Sadducees; and after the Pharisees carried the day they placed special stress on the function of the *Midrash* in creating new rules of Halakha,[2] but they continued to maintain the superiority of Halakha proper. Thus it was accepted in the schools that when confronted with "Halakha and *Midrash* one should attend to the Halakha" (T Sanhedrin VII 7).

Before long the functions of the scribe ceased to be the prerogative of the Levites, and they were given to the Sages regardless of descent. Ecclesiasticus (XXXII 16) speaks of those "that fear the Lord" who "shall find judgment", and not only of the house of Aaron and the house of Levi. Originally, perhaps, they sat together in the schools and in the courts : priests, Levites and other Israelites, and the *Midrash* would take form by the consent of all.

Midrash was conceived not only within the frame of study of Torah but also within cases tried according to the Torah. After the witnesses

---

[1] Epstein, Talm. Lit. 501-520. Not everything in our Midrash, however, belongs to the early interpretation.

[2] Urbach, in Tarbiz (Hebrew) XXVII (1957/8), 166 ff. As to the system of the Midrash see also I.L. Seeligmann, VT Suppl. I (1953) 150 ff.; R. Bloch, Dict. de la Bible, Suppl. V (1957) 1263 ff.; F. Maas, Zeitschrift für Theologie und Kirche LII (1955) 129-161; M. Eschelbacher, MGWJ LXVIII (1924) 47 ff.; 126 ff.; and also S. Bialoblocki, *s.v. Hermeneutik*, Encyclopaedia Judaica VII 1181-94; de Vries, History, 9-21; as to Maimonides' system see J. Neubauer, Maimonides on the Words of the Scribes (Hebrew), Jerusalem, 1957.

were examined and the facts verified "they would discuss the passage
bearing on the case all night, and if he was a murderer they would
discuss the passage concerning the murderer, and if he had committed
incest they would discuss the passage concerning incest" (T Sanhedrin
IX 1). In this way they pronounced judgment according to Midrash
and created new rules of Halakha.[1]

It may be assumed that the *teacher of merit* was a judge proving by
Scripture that the accused should be acquitted, and the *teacher of
fault* was one who proved the contrary. There may have been a meeting
of teaching in the academy and teaching of merit in concrete cases,
when cases were tried in the supreme court according to the decrees
of the Sadducees, that is to say in the closing days of John Hyrcanos
or in the days of King Jannaeus. At that time it was usual to administer
the law with rigour, contrary to the spirit of the Pharisaic sages, and
it was perhaps on such occasions that part of the rules of Halakha
were enuntiated which were calculated to interpret the criminal law
of the Torah as restrictively as possible, by making guilt depend on
certain conditions.[2] The Pharisees, in this way, showed that the Sadduceean court in effect shed blood.

Originally every verse of Scripture was interpreted independently,
until there were formulated *categories for expounding the Torah*, whose
number reached seven at the time of Hillel. Some of these categories
were apparently adopted by the Sages before the Hasmonean revolt,
following prototypes derived from Greek rhetoric,[3] but were afterwards considered Halakha handed down by tradition from Moses on
Sinai.[4]

3. Oral Law.

At the side of the *written law* there slowly came into being the *oral
law*, which was studied in the academy either together with the written

---

[1] Albeck, Introduction 42; cf. Ecclesiasticus **XXXII** 23.

[2] For instance M Sanhedrin VII 8-9.

[3] As to the categories and their relationship to the Greek rhetors D. Daube, HUCA
(1949) 239 ff; *id*. Festschrift H. Lewald, Basel 1953, 27 ff; *id*. The NT and Rabbinic
Judaism, London 1956, 63ff., 86 ff.; *id*. Jewish Journal of Sociology III (1961) 3 ff.;
Lieberman, Hellenism 68 ff.; S. Zeitlin, JQR LIV (1963-64) 161 ff.

[4] As to the Midrash see further : J. Neubauer, Sinai (Hebrew) XXII (1947/8), 49-80;
F. Maas, Zeitschrift für Theologie und Kirche LII (1955) 153 ; B. Cohen, Law and Tradition, 6 ff.; *id*. JRL 31 ff.; Wright, CBQ XXVIII (1966) 417 ff.

law or apart from it.[1] Even though there were many people who knew
how to read and write, and they were in possession of books, deeds
and other documents, in the academy no use was made of books. At
first there was a feeling that " of making many books there is no end
(Ecclesiastes XII 12), and it was held that "things taught orally may
not be said in writing" (TB Gittin 60b), so that the new books should
not be considered part of Scripture.[2] For this very reason, later on,
the Sadducees denied the validity of the oral law.[3] Moreover there may
have been an intention to limit the knowledge of the oral law to members of the schools, and to avoid publicizing the "mysteries" to the
common people.[4]

Another reason why the *oral law* was learnt in this fashion was the
duty of every scholar who brought to the school a tradition he had heard
(*shmu'a*) to deliver it orally, as described in the tractate Eduyoth.[5]
He had to specify the name of the person who had said it, and if
possible to name all the scholars who by handing it down from mouth
to mouth constituted its chain of descent.[6] On such an occasion he
would have to stand examination on the part of the members of the
school, just as if he were a witness; and since the rule regarding witnesses is "from their own mouth and not from that of their writing" (TB
Yebamoth 31b), it was required that new rules of Halakha be introduced orally and not in writing.[7]

---

[1] As to the oral law, see : J.N. Epstein, Introduction to the Version of the Mishna
(Hebrew), 693 ff., *id*. Tannaitic Lit. 16 ff.; I. Baer, Zion (Hebrew) XXVII (1961/2),117 ff.;
A.J. Heschel, Torah from Heaven in Historical Perspective (Hebrew), London 1962-5,
A. Goldberg, Maḥanayim (Hebrew) 112, 1967; Albeck, Introduction, 3; Cohen, JRL,
5 f., B. Gerhardsson, Memory and Manuscript, Copenhagen, 1964; Lieberman, Hellenism,
83 ff.; G. Weil, MGWJ LXXXIII (1939) 239-260.

[2] If the Mishna were written on the Torah, the copier might include it in the text
proper, as apparently happened to the Samaritan Torah and in many books of Halakha
and Agadah. In practice, however, even halakha was written down for private use,
though in the academy it was recited orally.

[3] Josephus, Antiquities XIII, 10, 6, 297

[4] Gerhardsson, 158; Albeck, Introduction, 115; B. de Vries, Introduction 62 ff.
A considerable part of the Halakha such as the laws of presumptions and reliability,
is only suitable for parties who are not versed in the law.

[5] See M Aboth VI 6; A Perles, MGWJ LVIII (1914) 311 ff.

[6] Albeck, Introduction, 94.

[7] As to the parallism with Greek Law : Jones, Law, 62. The parallel concept in Muslim
law to the chain of descent referred to is the *isnad*—J. Horovitz, Der Islam VIII (1918)
39 ff., J. Robson, Transactions of Glasgow University Oriental Soc. XV (1955) 15 ff.,
W. Bacher, Die Exegetische Terminologie der jüdischen Traditionsliteratur, Leipzig
1905 I, Tradition u. Tradenten in Schulen Palästinas und Babyloniens, Leipzig 1914.

Synonyms for oral law are *shmu'a* (i.e. that which was heard, tradition), *mishna, halakha, kabbala* (i.e. that which was accepted), and *words of the Scribes*.[1] In the Epistle of Aristeas (127), referring to observation of the commandments, it is said that "this is attained more by hearing than by reading", in other words, that in determining halakha the oral tradition is more important than the written law. Study in the school was based mainly on oral traditions, as is evidenced by such expressions as "... if they *heard* it-they told them" (M Sanhedrin XI 2), "I *heard* from the mouth of many" (M Eduyoth V 7), "they did not insist on their own words when confronted with an oral tradition" (T Eduyoth I 3). Hence oral tradition is accepted, in the rules of procedure of the schools, as a basis for putting a rule of Halakha to the vote (T Sanhedrin VII 2).[2]

The Sadducees objected to rules of Halakha originating from oral tradition, as Josephus says, "since the Pharisees handed down to the people a number of rules of halakha by tradition of the fathers, which were not written in the law of Moses, and therefore the Sadduceean sect rejects them, holding that only those that are written should be considered to be laws, whereas those derived from tradition of the fathers need not be observed" (Antiquities, XIII, 10, 6, 297).

Even the Pharisees felt that oral tradition at times overstepped its bounds, and in this respect they perhaps accepted some of the Sadduceean criticism. "Release of vows is floating in the air, having *nothing to lean on*...[3] they are like mountains suspended on a hair, of little Scripture and a multitude of halakha" (M Ḥagiga I 8). Even in the days of the Amoraim, (i.e. the sages of 200-500 C.E.) the commandments admitted by the Sadducees were deemed to be of greater effect than mere oral traditions (TB Sanhedrin 33b).

However in discussing the rules of oral tradition the Pharisees were strict precisely in these matters, in order "to desillusion the Sadducees" (TB Makkoth 5b). Thus it was said "there is a severity in the *words of the scribes* above that of the *words of the Torah* : (an elder) who says there is no (commandment of) Tefillin... is not guilty; (if he says there are) five compartments...[4] he is guilty" (M Sanhedrin XI 3).

---

[1] The author may have been following Plato and Aristotle, who defined study as listening and not as reading. Jones, Law, 11 f.

[2] W. Bacher, Tradition, 9 ff.

[3] Cf. Aboth III 16, where the same term refers to the validity of contract.

[4] There have recently been discovered in the Judean Desert Phylacteries including a compartment with the Ten Commandments; see Sifre Wa'ethannan 35 on the expression "and thou shalt bind them"— .... The Ten Commandments, which were not pre-

Words of the Scribes here are equivalent to *words of the sages* (cf. TJ Yebamoth II 4, 3d and TB *ibid.* 20a), and thus they include all the laws *of the Sages* or to use the Aramaic terms, common to the Amoraim, *derabanan* (i.e. of our rabbis) as distinct from *de'oraitha* (i.e. of the Torah). Obviously in the matter of the defiant elder, where the purpose of the law was to impose the authority of the sages on those who tended to deny it, the attitude was one of severity regarding rabbinical law even more than that regarding outright Scripture, as there was no danger that the express words of the Torah would be rejected.[1]

The parallel term *halakha* serves in at least four meanings. First, it denotes the decision of a dispute, that is to say, the way, in which one should walk, chosen between the two alternative ways. Second, it refers to the duty which we owe to the Almighty—and the law that He decreed. Third, the term *halakha* may be used to describe laws not expressly mentioned in scripture, either such as we regard as *halakha of Moses from Sinai* or such as we distinguish from reasoned law (*din*) : If it is *halakha* we will accept it, but if it is derived from reasoning, it can be refuted (M Yebamoth VIII 3).[2] Finally, *halakha* is the product of the schools as distinct from actual custom, and in this meaning the Palestinian scholars used the expressions *halakha* and *ma'aseh* (i.e. act) to distinguish between *a priori* and *a posteriori*, thus, it is sometimes noted that a certain law is "*halakha* but not implemented" or that "custom supersedes *halakha*". The common element in all these meanings is that they refer to oral law, and the introduction of the concept of *halakha* goes back to the Pharisees.

4. PROPHECY

Although teaching the laws and the Torah was a function of the

---

ceded by other commandments, should not they have to be bound ? .... As to this, Scripture says "and thou shalt bind them"—it is them that thou shalt bind and not the Ten Commandments". There may have been a case of a recalcitrant elder precisely in the matter of phylacteries and that the Pharisees endeavoured to reject opinions such as those of the scribes whose phylacteries have been found in the Judean Desert. As to these phylacteries and the difference between them and the Talmudical halakha see K.G. Kuhn, Phylakterien aus Höhle 4 von Qumran, Abhandl. der Heidelberger Akademie der Wissenschaften, Phil. Hist. Kl. 1957, 1, 24-31 ; and also Y. Yadin, Ma'ariv (Hebrew) 17.1.1969, and in Ereş Israel (Hebrew) 9, 1969.

[1] See Lieberman, Hellenism, 83.

[2] Cf.: "Here it is said as *halakha*, and here it is said as a *word of Torah*" (TJ Kethuboth I 1, 24d) And see p. 26 ff.

priests in the days of the First Temple, law was at times given by superhuman means, by the *Urim* and *Thummim* or through a prophet :
A prophet will the Lord thy God raise up unto thee, from the midth
of thee, of thy brethren, like unto me, unto him you shall hearken"
(Deut XVIII 15).[1]

In the days of the Second Temple instruction would be asked of
the priests (Haggai II 11) or of the prophet and the priest together
(Zechariah VII 3). Hence the laws of the Lord were considered such as
"He set before us by His servants the prophets" (Daniel IX 10).
Consulting the prophet became important when the Urim and Thummim ceased, yet at times it was thought that their end meant in effect
that the divine will could no longer be ascertained. It was thus decided,
in regard to priests who could not find their genealogical register, "that
they should not eat of the most holy things, till there stood up a priest
with *Urim* and with *Thummim*" (Ezra II 63)—with no mention of the
Prophet.[2]

As the Sages ascribed to the Prophets authority to instruct halakha
they also attributed to them authority to declare leap years and
determine the calendar, a function belonging to the Sanhedrin. It was
thus said that Elisha declared a leap year (T Sanhedrin II 9), and
so also Jeremiah and Ezekiel (TJ Sanhedrin I 2, 19a). Statutes and
customs were similarly ascribed to prophets (M Ta'anith IV 2, Yadayim
IV 3; T Erubin VIII (XI) 22) and the *prophets* were counted as a
link in the chain of tradition between the *Elders*, who survived Joshua,
and the *Men of the Great Synagogue* (M Aboth I 1). It is for this reason
that the books of the Prophets were expounded and served as a source
for Halakha.[3]

A Midrash found in Sifre on the above quotation from Deut. may
possibly be attributed to an early period : "A prophet... from the midst
of thee... unto him ye shall hearken—even if he tells you to contravene
any of the commandments mentioned in the Torah as did Elijah on
Mount Carmel—hearken to him". Only later on were the words *"for*

---

[1] As to halakha and prophecy : E.E. Urbach, Tarbiz (Hebrew) XVIII (1946/7) 1-27.
Obviously, prophecy in the main does not deal halakhic detail but rather to morals
and to duty, but the prophet at times was called upon to lay down the law.

[2] Although there apparently were prophets in those days, as Prof. J.M. Grinz remarks
to me (cf. Neh. VI 7, 12, 14), in matters of priesthood the prophet was not relied on.

[3] See Urbach *ibid.* and also Alon, Studies II 233 ; de Vries, Intro., 42.

the time being" added in order to restrict the prophet's authority.[1] The Samaritans on their part, and perhaps also the Sadducees and other sects, denied all such authority of the prophets, relying on the words of their Torah and book of Joshua.[2] In that period there was not yet need to conceal the book of Ezekiel (cf. TB Shabbath 13b), even though it contains contradictions of the Torah. The phrase used by Hillel indicates the legitimate status of the prophet : "They said to him, how should the people act who did not bring knives and paschal lambs to the temple. He said to them, the holy spirit is upon them, if they are not prophets they are the *sons of prophets"* (T Pasḥa IV 14 (2)).

Henceforth various rules of halakha were made as temporary measures only, as it was no longer possible to refer matters to a prophet : "And they set down the stones on the temple mountain at a reserved place until a *prophet* would come to instruct them (I Maccabees IV 46),[3] "and the Jews and the priests agreed that Simeon be their prince and high priest forever until there arise a true *prophet"* (I Maccabees XIV 41). It was perhaps at this time that such rules of halakha were made as "if he finds ... articles of gold or of glass ... let him not touch them *until Elijah comes"*(M Baba Meṣia II 8) or "if two deposit in the hands of one ... the rest shall remain *until Elijah comes"*(M Baba Meṣia III 4).[4]

Similarly opinion was split as to whether superhuman evidence for halakha should be adduced : "The House of Shammai say : No testimony may be given of a *divine voice*, and the House of Hillel say : Testimoney may be given of a *divine voice"* (T Neziruth I 1),[5] and in like manner R. Eliezer and R. Joshua disagreed as to whether attention should be given to a *divine voice* or similar signs (TB Baba Meṣia 59b), and it is remarkable that R. Eliezer relies on a *divine voice* whereas R. Joshua rejects it.

The early Christians, as we know, relied on their prophet in order

---

[1] In its present form this Midrash contains a change in direction of thought. At its beginning it stresses the authority of the prophet : "even if he tells you" ... and at the end it stresses his limitations : "for the time being". Hence the second part seems to be an addition.

[2] The Sages also said : "If Israel had not sinned they would not have been given any more than the Torah and the Book of Joshua" (TB Nedarim 22b)—meaning that these are of special importance.

[3] Cf. Hoenig, Sanh., 39 n. 12.

[4] I assume that the expression is much older than the literary text including it.

[5] Cf. T. Sotah XIII 2.

to change matters of Halakha, and they adduced authority for so doing mainly from the books of the prophets. The Sages, on the other hand, stressed the rational system, which substitutes the scholar for the prophet. "These are the commandments which the Lord commanded Moses—from now on *a prophet may not innovate*" (Sifra, end of Lev.).[1] As a result of this approach R. Joshua denied the validity of R. Eliezer's proof, and in accordance with this way of thinking there was a plan to conceal the book of Ezekiel. There were also some of the Sages who held that the words of the prophets are not for practical application (TB Niddah 23a) and that only the words of the written or oral law may be relied upon.[2]

5. Precedent

Some rules of Halakha are based on cases which occurred and on instructions given by the Sages on concrete occasions. An outstanding example is the halakha regarding a woman who claims that her husband died and seeks permission to remarry. There was a case of a woman who went with her husband to the harvest and came and said : *My husband has died;* and the Sages said : Let her marry. From this case the House of Shammai concluded, by way of extension, that also " a woman who comes from overseas and says : *My husband has died*—may marry, *My husband has died*—may be taken to wife by the husband's brother. For the House of Shammai hold : the same law applies whether she comes from the harvest or from the olives or from overseas, they only mentioned the harvest because this was the actual case" (M Eduyoth I 12). The dispute turned on the extent of the permission rule that may be deducted from the case and it was remarkably the House of Shammai that chose the more liberal path and the House of Hillel were stricter in this regard.

To cases such as this testimony was given in the schools, and if

---

[1] See Urbach, 7-8. In accordance with this latter-day rule of halakha the law relating to the false prophet was extended to include not only a person who would abolish the prohibition of idolatry but also a person who would abolish any one of the other commandments : TB Sanhedrin 90a.

[2] As to the attitude of the Sages to miracles see I. Heinemann, in B. Heller Jubilee Vol. Budapest 1941, 170 ff.; A. Guttmann, HUCA XX (1947) 363 ff. Words of *Kabbala* (Acceptance) include the books of the Prophets and the Hagiographa, apparently on account of the chain of descent at the beginning of M Aboth, where the prophets are mentioned as those who accepted the law from the "Elders".

the words of the scholar were intrinsically sound the case turned into a precedent. Thus there testified R. Ḥanania the Prefect of Priests "to a small village that was at the side of Jerusalem, and a certain old man lived there and he used to make loans to all the villagers and write in his own handwriting and others would sign (i.e. as witnesses) and a case came before the Sages and they allowed it.[1] By the same token a woman may write her own bill of divorcement, and a man may write his own receipt, since a document is only constituted by its signatories" (M Eduyoth II 3).

Similarly there was adduced "a case when Ben-Zakkai examined concerning stalkes of figs", from which there was gathered a rule in examining witnesses : "whoever goes into greater detail in examining witnesses is praiseworthy" (M Sanhedrin V 2).

It may be assumed that halakhic provisions of the Mishna recorded anonymously and followed by a case are gathered from the case, which in fact preceded them.[2] Perhaps even such provisions as are recorded in casuistic terms indicate that they are based on cases. Examples to this are the provisions opening with the words "He who ..." hinting that there was a case in point although no need was seen to report it in so many words after the halakha.

6. Custom

Custom is recognized as a source for the formation of rules of behaviour to the extent that they have not crystallized according to halakha in one of the other ways indicated. It is sometimes said that in a place where there exists a custom to do a certain thing there is a duty to do it. On such occasions the Mishna refers to matter not yet regulated by halakha, in other words to a custom filling a legal void. Even in regard to commandments of the Torah terms denoting custom are used to indicate their binding nature, which in turn is revealed by the custom. A certain commandment may be said to be "*customary*" both within and without the Land of Israel, or whether or not the

---

[1] In other words, they gave effect to the bill, and from this case they inferred as to bills of divorcement, where the term "allow" more properly applies. It therefore appears that the expression "they allowed" was initially used when a bill of divorcement was considered, and then it was applied also to the source, which deals with the promissory note.

[2] Albeck, Introduction 92. Cf. also Tchernowitz, History, Pt. 1, 189, de Vries, History 169; E.Z. Melamed, Sinai (Hebrew) XLVI (1959/60), 152-166.

temple is functioning. In the primary meaning of the expression, we are supposed to investigate what the custom of the public is, in order to know how far the application of a commandment extends, and there can be no greater recognition of the force of custom.[1]

It may be assumed that the importance of custom was greater in so far as the oral law was not yet developed and sources of halakha were not yet available. It also stands to reason that the force of custom was greater outside Jerusalem than in a place of Torah from which Torah went forth. The area outside Jerusalem or outside the Temple was called the *country* (M Ma'aser Sheni III 4, Rosh Hashana IV 1), and it therefore seems likely that the rule "everything according to the *custom of the country*" was first aired outside Jerusalem. In this rule there is also an attempt to reconcile conflicting sources : the Sage confronted with contradictory rules of Mishna attributed the fact to local customs.

Local custom is sometimes also referred to as *halakhoth of the country* as distinct from the halakha going forth from Jerusalem and based on Midrash of the Torah or on statutes of a court : "Keepers of produce eat (of it) pursuant to *halakhoth of the country* but not pursuant to the Torah" (M Baba Meṣia VII 8). In this instance the function assigned to custom was in the nature of a reform and not merely of a topgap, for if the keeper may not eat according to the Torah his eating is tantamount to theft and thus forbidden. The custom of the country in effect permits what is forbidden according to the Torah, and thus finds itself reforming the halakha. However this custom is not binding in itself, but it becomes an implied term in the agreement between the owner of the field and the keeper. It is similar to a custom which a court has decreed to be binding or has acted according to it. Anyhow the wording of the Mishna points to a divergence between the Torah and the custom, and from there is only one step to the principle *custom supersedes halakha*.

This principle, mentioned in TJ Yebamoth XII 1, 12c,[2] and Baba Meṣia VII 1, 11b, refers to two concrete cases. One is a decision concerning *prohibition and permission* [3] and the other is a matter of civil law regarding the relationship of employer and employee. Again the custom in the former case has only a function of deciding, since it

---

[1] Cf. T Ta'aniyoth II 5 preserving the original meaning of *noheg*.

[2] And in TB Yebamoth 102a.

[3] I.e. matters of ritual as the ceremony of *unshoeing* (Deut. XXIV 9).

relies on the view of a number of sages,[1] but it does not go against commonly accepted halakha. And the second case also merely shows the effect of custom in filling out terms of an agreement, on the assumption that the parties agreed to act according to local custom. So no ground is furnished for the idea that custom really supersedes halakha in torts or in *prohibition and permission*.

However the generalized formula *custom supersedes halakha* bears looking into. Perhaps it was accepted in principle among circles who opposed halakha, maybe among the unlearned inhabitants of the countryside, who tried to reject the demands of the sages and relied on their own custom. In the days of the Amoraim word of this principle reached the schools, and authority for it was sought in the halakha itself.

Insofar as the Sages predominated, the effect of custom was restricted, and its place was taken by halakha. A case in point is that of the "congregation in Tiberias, where the public took a permissive view, until Rabban Gamliel and the Elders came and restrained them" (M Erubin X 10). The critical approach to customs grew stronger, so much so that in the course of discussion of the rules regarding reading the Scroll of Esther in the Tractate of Sopherim XIV 18, the following words are used : "This was the custom of the people, as halakha is not determined until there is a custom. This is the meaning of the expression *custom supersedes halakha*—custom of the Elders;[2] but custom for which there is no evidence from the Torah is like a mere *injudicious decision*". In other words, halakha set forth by the Sages is binding if it has spread in Israel like a custom,[3] it cannot, however be superseded by custom but only by proof from the Torah or by a decision of the elders.

Such a formula appears, indeed, only in the post-talmudic period, but the criticism of custom that it contains is much older, as the case of Rabban Gamliel and the Elders shows. Further, it is evidenced also by the expression *condition of the Court*. At least in some of the

---

[1] de Vries, History 162, and see *ibid.* further studies and literature concerning custom, 157-168. As to custom in general see also A. Perles, Festschrift Israel Lewy, Breslau 1911, 66-75; A. Guttmann, MGWJ XXXIII (1939) 226-38; Tchernowitz, History I, 144-150; Alon, Studies II, 242; M. Vogelman, Sinai (Hebrew) XVII (1945), 362-373. As to custom in Hellenistic Law, R. Taubenschlag, JJP I (1946) 41-54.

[2] Hebrew *watiq* has been derived from Greek *eutikos* : J. Levy, Wörterbuch über die Talmudim², 1924

[3] Cf. Maimonides, Hilkhoth Mamrim, 2, 2.

cases where this expression occurs it denotes a custom and not a statute, referring to an implied condition in an agreement between two parties. Instead of attributing such a condition to the custom of the people and calling it a *common condition* it was attributed to the Court, in order to stress that recourse to custom may be had only if a Court has agreed to it.

7. ACCEPTANCE (*kabbala*)

In the writings of Josephus and in the Gospels the term *paradosis* (i.e. that which has been received, tradition) denotes the oral law. In Talmudic use *words of kabbala* are such as belong to the post-Pentateuchal parts of the Bible. In our context the term has a completely different meaning, that of one of the ways of creating obligations and rules of halakha.[1]

An instance of a decision taken by the people in matters of halakha is found in Esther IX, 27 (whether the decision was in fact taken is a question which need not be entered upon here) : "The Jews ordained, and took upon (*kibbelu*) them, and upon their seed, and upon all such as joined themselves unto them, so as it should not fail, that they would keep these two days according to the writing thereof, and according to the appointed time thereof, every year". The I Book of Maccabees, IV 58, uses the same style in describing the decision concerning Ḥanukka.

These decisions are the creations of a *Great Assembly* in which the patriarchal heads of families took part, and they were recorded for time in writing or inscribed in stone. The decisions derived their force from the will of the people, and going on the premise that a community never dies it was possible to impose duties on generations to follow as well.

Other examples of the activity of the people in assembly are the acceptance of the Torah in the time of Ezra, the pact concluded in the time of Neḥemia and perhaps the statutes of the *Men of the Great Synagogue*.[2] In fact the decisions were prepared by individuals, and the assembly was convened for purposes of publication only, but in

---

[1] Cf. S. Atlas, HUCA XXVI (1955) 1-38 and I. Baer, Zion (Hebrew) XV (1949/50), 1-41. *Kabbala* here serves in the same meaning as *haskamah* (agreement) in the communities of Spain, and corresponds with *conventional law*.

[2] Perhaps certain implied terms "in consideration of which Joshua caused Israel to inherit the land" (TB Baba Kama 80b) were also proclaimed in this way.

theory the statute emanated from the people itself, and its binding element was its *confirmation* and *acceptance*. These two terms apparently refer to the oath or ban declared on the occasion. At a certain stage the decision no longer came forth from the public but was instead pronounced by the Sages. However the presence of the public was required to publish the halakha and to give it effect, and for this reason Samuel (the Amora) used to gather the people in order to declare rules of halakha (TB Kethuboth 7b).

In practice not all the men appeared at the usual assemblies but only the princes and the elders, and their decision bound the whole community. Ezra X, 7-8, has this to say of the general assembly : "And they made proclamation throughout Judah and Jerusalem unto all the children of the captivity, that they should gather themselves together unto Jerusalem, and that whosoever came not within three days, according to the counsel of the princes and the elders, all his goods be forfeited, and himself separated from the congregation of the captivity".

Relics from the creation of halakha by *acceptance* may be found in a number of contexts. Though it was forbidden for single officials of the temple to dominate the public, there were certain officials who pointed out that the rule did not apply to them, "as they had been *accepted by the majority* of the public" (M Shekalim V 2). Recourse to public consent was taken also in regard to certain acts of the Sanhedrin. Leap years are declared, and all public business is attended to, only conditionally, so that the majority of the public may accept (T Sanhedrin II 13).[1] It was thus said in Palestine : "Any decree, imposed on the public by a court, which has not been *accepted* by the majority of the public, is no decree"—(TJ Shabbath I 7, 3d ; Aboda Zara II 9, 41d). On the other hand the scholars of Babylon were more removed from democratic concepts, and their version was : "No decree may be imposed on the public unless the majority of the public *can endure it*" (TB Aboda Zara 36a).[2]

Besides the general rules of halakha that were accepted there were also such that only certain groups accepted, in addition to the law or instead of it. The groups of Ḥassidim, Pharisees and Essenes pre-

---

[1] And compare the formula "on condition that the prince so wishes"; Sinai (Hebrew) LIV (1963/64), 341.

[2] This is an objective criterion to be used by the Sages at their judicious discretion, whereas the criterion in TJ is subjective and is vested in the public itself. On the process of decline of democracy see Alon, Studies, II, 15 ff.

scribed commandments each for themselves, imposed by general
assembly, similarly to the proceeding indicated above. Joining anyone
of these groups involved acceptance of such commandments as described in M Demai II 2-3 : "A person undertaking to be a *trusted
person* tithes what he eats and what he sells and what he buys, and does
not stay at the home of an unlearned person ..., a person undertaking
to be an *associate* does not sell an unlearned person liquids or solids
and does not buy from him liquids, and does not stay at the home of
an unlearned person, and does not entertain him in his own garment".

The ceremony of acceptance is discussed in T Demai II 2-19, and
among other things the following was laid down : "A person wishing
to *accept*, even a scholar must *accept*, but a scholar who is a regular
member of a school need not *accept*, because he *accepted* when he first
joined the school". In the Dead Sea sect the commandments were
discussed and determined in the *public assembly;* the *Manual of
Discipline* and the *Damascus Covenant* are collections of decisions
adopted by this Session. Here, too, there is a fixed procedure for
acceptance of the commandments on the part of an individual joining
the community.[1]

Trade and neighbourhood groupings also made regulations for themselves. We are told of binding decisions on the part of people living
in the same courtyard, or the same city, or on the part of wool-dealers,
painters, bakers, donkey-drivers and seamen, and the sages recognized
the binding effect of such agreements as if they were made in pursuance
of the Torah (T Baba Meṣia XI 22-26).[2]

8. COMPROMISE

When a doubt arose in a civil matter there was sometimes created
halakha by compromise. Such a solution may first perhaps been chosen
by lay judges, who were not learned enough to give judgment according to halakha sources. They would conciliate the litigants and impose
a compromise upon them.[3] Henceforth the method was at times

---

[1] See. Rabin, QS 1 ff., 106 ff.

[2] As to regulations of the townsmen see infra, and as to regulations of tradesmen see
RIDA XVI (1969), 11-19. As to the regulations of the Ḥasidim : B. de Vries Memorial
Volume (Hebrew), Jerusalem, 1968, 62-69.

[3] As to lay judges : Alon, Studies, II, 15 ff.: as to compromise see also Cohen, JRL
654 ff. As to the imposition of a compromise as a first stage in Ptolemaic law, see E. Seidl,
PtRG 86, 89.

adopted in halakha, although originally the Sages objected to a solution harming the party in the right.

An instance of this is the case of the widow who died while awaiting the coming of age of her husband's brother and her estate was claimed by the heirs of both her husband and herself : "The House of Shammai say, let the heirs of the husband *divide* with those of the father" (M Yebamoth IV 3). A similar doubt exists when a house collapses on a person and the person whom he was to succeed; and the heir of each claims that the one who died last was the person whom he was to succeed : "The House of Shammai say, let them *divide*" (M Baba Bathra IX, 8-9). In both these cases the House of Hillel preferred the legal solution *"property remains as it was"*, whereas the House of Shammai may have been in awe of deciding and therefore chose the solution of compromise.

Parallel terms in this regard are *making a compromise* (M Kethuboth X 6; T Baba Kama II 10), *"breaking in the middle"* (T Sanhedrin I 2-3), and *"dividing* between the parties" (M Baba Bathra VII 4).

In the course of time this method became more widely adopted, and it was attributed to Aaron the priest, who was " a lover of peace and a pursuer of peace" (TB Sanhedrin 6b). The contrary method was attributed to Moses and was typified by the expression "let the law *penetrate the mountain"* referring apparently to the case of partition between partners where a mountain stands where the new boundary is to pass : the man standing on his right and opposing any compromise demands that a hole be drilled into the mountain for the boundary to be drawn through it.[1]

We thus find division adopted as a regular solution by the Sages in quite a number of cases, for instance : "Two men holding a garment ... let them *divide"* (M Baba Meṣia, I 1), "A cow which was exchanged for a donkey and gave birth ... the one says—before I sold, and the other says—after I bought : let them *divide"* (M Baba. Meṣia VIII 4), or in more general terms in the doctrine of Symmachos "Property cast in doubt is to be *divided"* (TB Baba Kama 46a).

9. Legal Fiction

The Torah being divine and immutable, there arose difficulties in the wake of the changing times and circumstances. The Pharisees and the

---

[1] Note by my student Mr. A. Horovitz.

Sages saw no way to change the halakha, especially where it originated in the Torah, and they therefore had recourse to legal fiction. Legal fiction denotes a legal assumption that a certain set of facts exists, although at variance with the truth; and proceeding upon such an assumption a rule of halakha is excluded from application, or a rule is applied which could only have effect in that set of facts.[1]

An example of this method is the abduction of the daughters of Shiloh, which was designed to circumvent the oath and to make the intermarriage with the tribe of Benjamin possible (Judges XXI 16-23). The more the laws of the Torah were implemented in the days of the Second Temple the greater was the need for similar means to adhere to the theory that the Torah does not change and yet to facilitate certain changes in practice.

The idea of the *Prosbol* introduced by Hillel rests on the principle of fiction. Hillel did not wish to abolish the law of the seventh year release, but he wanted to enable lenders to collect their debts after the seventh year too. The bill of *Prosbol* purports to give notice to the Court that the creditor is about to collect the debt, and this is the first step toward collection by an officer of court or by the creditor with Court permission. The fiction lies in the fact that the bill is written already when the loan is made or before the release year, and not so as to begin collection but to circumvent the law of the release. Hillel "saw that the people abstained from lending to each other", and hence the need to enable loans to be made (M Shebi'ith X 3-4).[2]

Another example is the *transfer by incident* of title to chattel. According to halakha one may transfer title to a complete farm, and if the purchaser takes title to the land all the chattels on the premises become his. There occurred "a case of a certain man from Meron who was in Jerusalem and possessed many chattels of which he wanted to make a gift. He was told he could not as he had no land. He therefore bought a rock near Jerusalem and declared, the north part of this

---

[1] As to legal fiction in general: H. Maine, Ancient Law, London, ch. II; as to legal fiction in the ancient Orient: G. Boyer, RIDA I (1954) 73 ff.; and as to legal fiction in the Halakha: Tchernowitz, History I, 179-188; D. Askowith, Jewish Studies in memory of I. Abrahams, New York 1927, 1-11; J.S. Zuri, B.M. Levin Volume (Hebrew), Jerusalem 1940, 174-195; S. Goldman, Studia W.B. Stevenson, Glasgow University Oriental Society, 1945; S. Atlas, L. Ginzburg Volume (Hebrew), New York 1946, 1-24. As to legal fiction in Greek Law: Jones, Law, 305 ff.

[2] As to the Prosbol see L. Blau, Festschrift der Landesrabbinerschule, Budapest 1927; M. Ginsberg, Arctos III (1962), 37-44; J.Z. Cahana, Release of Money (Hebrew), Jerusalem, 1945.

and together with it one hundred head of sheep and one hundred barrels of wine are hereby given to X ... and the Sages upheld his words" (T Baba Bathra X 12). In this case the man had to be enabled to make a testament, and therefore they were willing to consider transfer of title to chattels in a distant town as if it were part of a transaction of transfer of a complete farm.

The collectors for the Temple used legal fiction in order to avoid injury to the Treasury. Although the Torah says that a person who made a vow to bring a sacrifice must do so *willingly* (Lev I 3), it was held that coercion is exercised. Could it possibly be perforce ? Thus we learn from the expression *Willingly*. How then ? Coercion is exercised until he says *I wish* (M Arakhin V 6).

Opposition to the use of legal fictions was indeed voiced, and even from among the Sages themselves. A person who swore off anything would generally ask a scholar to release the vow, and he, in turn, would discover a certain fact, unknown at the time of the vow, due to which a way to retract the vow could be found. Thus the vow could be declared to have been mistakenly made. On this the Mishna says (Ḥagiga I 8) : "Releases of vows float in the air and have *nothing to stand on*".[1] A complaint about the use of legal fiction to avoid the obligations of gifts and tithes is given in the name of R. Judah ben Elai : "Come and see how far removed latter-day generations are from earlier generations. The earlier generations used to bring in harvests through the main gateways so that they should be chargeable with tithe; latter-day generations bring in their harvests by way of roofs, courtyards and enclosures so that they should be exempt from tithe" (TB Berakhoth 35b).[2]

10. Legislation

Most rules of Halakha referred as deriving "from the words of our Rabbis" and not attributed by midrash to Scripture (or so attributed by way of mere hint only,) are statutes made from time to time by the spiritual leadership of the Sages.[3] In this matter the Scribes, the

---

[1] Cf. *supra*, p. 1, note 3.

[2] For a contrary view see TJ Yebamoth IV, 12, 6b, that fiction is sometimes needed, as in the case of R. Tarfon in a year of draught.

[3] The division into *words of the torah* and *words of the rabbis* is, of course not of an early date. Some rules assigned to the former group are of a later date than those

Elders and the Sages activated the *Great Synagogue*, the *gerousia* or the *Sanhedrin*, as legislative bodies, setting down norms for the future and not as *post factum* judges. A considerable part of the halakha rules, even where not expressly so indicated, are reforms, but sages later on found ways to reinforce the words of their precursors, and ascribed their authority to an expression of the Torah, to a rule of halakha or to other sources.[1]

The earliest statutes were apparently decrees intended as a *fence for the Torah* (M Aboth I 1), but subsequently statutes were enacted in fields which the Torah did not deal with, for reasons of *ways of peace,*[2] public policy or the like. Large parts of the Mishna in the Orders on Women and Torts are statutes created in the days of the Second Temple, and the fact that they are given anonymously indicates their antiquity.[3]

The Sages of the Talmud ascribed certain statutes to Moses and other Biblical figures, in order to give them a firmer basis, although they have no mention in Scripture.[4] However there are other statutes whose ancestry traced back to Ezra[5] or to the Men of the Great Synagogue[6] may be accepted as historically founded in fact. It is also reasonably correct that the decree attributed to the Hasmonean Court against foreign women (TB Aboda Zara 36b) is part of the reforms introduced by Judah the Maccabee and his colleagues toward the *"re-instatement* of the law of the Torah"[7] and the punishment of the offenders (I Maccabees III 8)[8].

Simeon ben Shetaḥ is considered the father of the statute obliging the

---

assigned to the latter one. Cf. Albeck, Mishna Shabbat, Introduction; de Vries, History. 69.

[1] As to legislation see : M.A. Bloch, Einleitung zur Lehre von den Verordnungen (Hebrew), 1879-1905; N. Wahrmann, Sinai (Hebrew) LIII (1962/3), 50-58; de Vries, History, 96-114.

[2] This is a paraphrase of scripture, Proverbs III, 17 : "Her ways are ways of pleasantness and all her pathes are peace"; see S. Bachrach Memorial Volume, Jerusalem 1970 (Hebrew) 63-67.

[3] Z. Frankel, Ways of the Mishna, Tel Aviv 1959, (Hebrew) 29 ff.

[4] See Bloch, *ibid.* 287-289.

[5] Such as "courts sit on Monday and Thursday" and "pedlars may ply their trade in outlying townlets" (TB Baba Kama 82a, TJ Megilla IV 1, 75a).

[6] Following their maxim "make a fence for the Torah", such decrees as "prohibitions of commandment" regarding "second degrees of consanguinity by words of the scribes" may be attributed to them (M Yebamoth II 4).

[7] Megillath Ta'anith : "On the 24th (of Ab) we returned to our Law".

[8] Cf. M. Hengel, Die Zeloten, Leiden 1961, 157 ff.

bridgeroom to write in the marriage deed that all his property is surety for the sums stipulated in it (T Kethuboth XII 1), and it is perhaps based on a custom in Neo-Babylonian law.[1] At about the same time the statute or custom was adopted to stipulate 200 dinars for a virgin and 100 dinars for a widow (TB Kethuboth 10a). To the extent that these were statutes, they were decided upon in the Great Court headed by Simeon ben Shetaḥ, and therefore they bear his name.[2]

The same may be said of the two statutes of Hillel, regarding the *Prosbol* (M Shebiʻit X 3) and regarding paying money into court to redeem a house in a walled city (M Arakhin IX 4) : these were also adopted by the Sanhedrin under his leadership. A series of statutes from the end of the days of the Second Temple is contained in M Gittin IV and V and in T Gittin IV. There were according to M Kethuboth XIII 1 two *judges of decree* (*dayanei gezeiroth*) in Jerusalem (according to the Palestinian version—"*dayanei gezeiloth*)",[3] and they not only gave judgment *a posteriori* but also made decrees for the future. Perhaps their title indicated they could issue their decrees independently of any further act of the general court.

A statute might be at variance with the Torah law, and the question was not yet raised whether the Court had the power to disregard anything in the Torah (TB Gittin 36b). Thus, for instance, a bill of divorcement was given effect although by Torah law it was invalid (M Gittin IV 1), a widow was permitted to re-marry on the strenght of minimal evidence of her husband's death (M Yebamoth XVI 7)[4], and "whipping and other punishments were imposed beyond the letter of the law" (TB Yebamoth 90b).

Similar to the position of a statute of the Sages *vis-a-vis* a provision of the Torah was the position of a latter statute to a previous. In early times it was not yet held that "one Court cannot render void the words of another unless it is greater in wisdom and in number" (M Eduyoth

---

[1] Cf. Tarbiz (Hebrew) XXXVII (1967/8) 39-47.

[2] But see J. Efron, Doron, Studies in Classic Culture (Hebrew), Tel Aviv 1967, 173 ff., who ascribes all these accomplishments to the Sages mentioned, and not to the Sanhedrin, which in his opinion did not exist at the time. To my mind, even though the Sanhedrin was not mentioned by name, these judicial and legislative acts cannot be imagined except within the framework of an organized body.

[3] Also meaning decrees, cognate with the Arabic *gazala*, meaning to cut.

[4] It was only the Amoraim who felt that the "power to permit" exercized by their forerunners had to be justified by the theory that "a person who betrothes does so on authority of the Sages".

I 5) : in every generation the Court would enact whatever the times required. The question apparently arose when there was a tendency to abolish some of the strictures of the *Eighteen Matters* (see M Shabbath I 4), and the opponents argued that in their generation the Court was not as great in wisdom and in number as were their predecessors. The reply of the liberals was that the prohibition had not been generally adopted (TB Aboda Zara 36a). In the name of Samuel it was said that the rule applies to the *Eighteen Matters* only, other statutes being repealable (TJ Shabbath I, 3d).[1] Later on the words of the Sages once enacted became vested with the sanctity of words of the Torah, and subsequent generations were denied the power to repeal them. It was at this stage that the Mishna in Eduyoth quoted above was enunciated.

11. Reasoning

According to Proverbs II 8-9, wisdom is required "that it may guard the paths of justice, and preserve the ways of his godly ones. Then shalt thou understand righteousness and justice, and equity, yea, every good path".[2] Ecclesiasticus IV 15, similarly considers wisdom a source of law : "that giveth ear unto her shall judge the nations", and he goes on to distinguish between various kinds of wisdom, not all of which are conducive to doing justice : "there is an exquisite subtility [3] and the same is unjust, and there is one that perverteth favour to gain a judgment (XIX 25.) In the terminology of the Sages, wisdom stands for the oral law,[4] indicating one of the important ways of creating halakha.

This appellation of the oral law is probably connected with reasoning,[5] which serves both the Court and the School in discovering halakha. It was accordingly in this context that the *possessor of "shemu'oth"*, oral traditions which he heard, was contrasted with the *sage* who

---

[1] See Alon, Studies II, 244.

[2] Wisdom appears already in the time of the First Temple as a synonym for Torah' Jeremiah VIII 8, as Prof. J.M. Grinz remarks.

[3] Subtility here means wisdom, and cf. the Targum of "thy brother came with guile', (Genesis XXVII 35).

[4] Epstein, Tannaitic Lit., 16 ; Cohen, JRL, 281.

[5] As to reasoning—W. Bacher, Terminologie II, 129 ff. ; H. Klein, JQR XXXVIII (1947-8) 67 ff., XLIII (1952-3) 341 ff., L (1959-60) 124 ff., M. Eschelbacher MGWJ LXVIII (1924), 47 ff., 126 ff. ; L. Jacobs, Studies in Talmudic Logic and Methodology, London 1961.

would enunciate rules of halakha based on his own knowledge and reasoning (TB Pesaḥim 105b).

A synonym for reasoning is *din* (logic). There is a saying quoted from R. Simeon, "in this matter the attribute of logic is deficient" (T Yebamoth IX 3, Taharoth III 7), indicating that the rule under discussion cannot stand up to the criticism of reasoning. *Din* in this context is contrasted with *halakha;* it is the creation of logic, and it stands on a par with tradition and acceptance. This form is of special importance in the creation of civil law, for in this field there are not many scriptural provisions and logic is appropriate to determine relationships between individuals. Thus for the Palestinian Amoraim the expression *category of reasoning* connoted civil law, and this is what was meant by the assertion that "in matters of the category of reasoning, i.e. in property cases, the assumption that everything is similar to the majority was not followed" (TJ Baba Kama V 1, 4d).

Din connotes generalisation, for reasoning tends to erect rules for interpreting the Torah and determining halakha. A person calling a rule a *din* attributes it to reasoning. In this meaning of the term *din* it denotes one of the categories for expounding the Torah, the inference *a minori ad majus*, thus hinting that it is permissible to make an *a fortiori* deduction without authority of tradition (TB Pesaḥim 66a). Hillel already made use of such reasoning in his argumentation with the Sons of Betheira : "It is also an inference *a minori ad majus :* if the daily offering, default in respect of which is not punishable with cutting off from the congregation, supersedes the Shabbath, should not the paschal lamb, where such default is so punishable, supersede the Sabbath ?" (*ibid.*) Indeed reasoning is here adduced only as an additional argument, for its value is less than that of tradition or of *gezeira shawa*, (similar scriptural wording) one ot the categories of expounding, not applicable on the strength of mere reasoning. The colleagues of R. Simeon thus reply to his argument based on the inference *a minori ad majus :* "If it is *halakha* we will accept it, but if it is derived from *reasoning* it can be refuted" (M Yebamoth VIII 3).[1]

Although scripture may generally be interpreted according to *din* there yet are certain matters in regard which recourse may not be had to deduction by analogy and to the use of reasoning. These matters

---

[1] As to this rule see: A. Schwarz, Jahresbericht der theolog. Lehranstalt Wien XXIII (1916) 163 ff. ; W. Bacher, Terminologie I, 79 ff., II, 83 ff.

are *novelties*,[1] from which no rule may be gathered regarding similar matters : "The scribes introduced a *novelty* and I have nothing by which to explain (M Kelim XIII 7; Tebul Yom IV 6). This is a departure from reasoning, and in this way the concept is prevented from developing into a complete system.

In the ancient tradition there are already beginnings of rules created by reasoning.[2] One example may serve to illustrate the abstract and generalizing reasoning of the early sages. According to the ancient halakha, if "a city was occupied by a besieging army, all the women of priestly families are *disqualified*" (inter alia, from-eating of offerings due to the priests) (M. Kethuboth II 9).[3] On a certain occasion at the end of the days of the Second Temple it was said that if "a woman said, I have been captured yet I am pure—she may eat, for *the mouth that prohibited is the mouth that permitted*" (M Eduyoth III 6). Thus a rule was applied in this case derived from reasoning and logic.[4]

To edit the Mishna not according to scriptural sequence but according to topical order involved the use of reasoning. Moreover, the Tannaim, by use of reasoning, came to create *fathers* and *generations*, headings and derivatives, which means extending the specific laws of the Torah, to become general rules (as in M Baba Kama I 1). Mention has already been made of the "*categories* of expounding the Torah", and it need only be stressed here that the expounder endeavours to interpret a given word, wherever he finds it, in the same way [5]. He thus is bound to create a rule instead of relying on a multitude of instances.

Reasoning was also conductive to the comparison of matters with one another, letting clear case shed light on doubtful one. Thus in M Kethuboth I 6, the scholars of Jabne use the expressions "*your field has become eroded*" and "*purchase made upon a mistaken assumption*" in describing arguments between husband and wife. They repre-

---

[1] A penalty is a *novelty* in this context, as distinct from restitution which is based on reasoning.

[2] The main rules and most use of reasoning, date from the time of the Amoraim : see Cohen, JRL, 480, 786.

[3] This rule of halakha was apparently laid down at the end of the reign of John Hyrcanus, in connection with the dispute between the king and the Pharisees : TB Qiddushin 66a.

[4] The reasoning that "the mouth that prohibited is the mouth that permitted" was later adopted in civil law : "And R. Joshua concedes that if a person tells another, 'This field belonged to your father and I bought it from him', he may be depended upon, for the mouth that prohibited is the mouth that permitted" (M Kethuboth II 2).

[5] Ch. Albeck, Untersuchungen über die halakhischen Midraschim, Berlin 1927, 1 f.

sent rules adopted from the field of civil to that of matrimonial law, due to their general logical application.[1]

12. RIGHT AND GOOD

The Sages clung to certain principles beyond formal halakha, such as *the right in the eyes of Heaven* (Sifre, Re'eh 79, 96) or *within the line of law* (Mekhiltha de-Amalek 4). The first of these concepts places Heavenly judgment above the laws obtaining in terrestrial courts, indicating that not everything permitted by halakha is right in the eyes of Him on high. This opens a way to reforms in the law such as are known to other legal systems. Compromise has already been mentioned above as one of the sources of law, and it probably grew out of rules similar to those under discussion here.

One who knows what is good *in the eyes of Heaven* is not bound by halakha alone, and may decide according to his own discretion. This was important when halakha was taking definite shape and the discretion of the judges was being restricted. It was then necessary to appeal to a Heavenly norm, in order to redress any wrong which might result from rigid application of bare halakha. It may be that this principle was first applied by arbitrators, who were not from among the scholars of halakha, or by the Hassidim, who were severe with themselves.[2]

The obligation *to fulfil one's duty towards Heaven* was invoked in the case of injury or death caused by an agent : "He who sets fire by the hand of a deaf-mute, an imbecile or a minor—is not liable by laws of man, but is liable by the *laws of Heaven*"(M Baba Kama VI 4) : according to ancient halakha it is impossible to give judgment against the principal, but he was told that he would not be fulfilling his duty towards Heaven until he remedied the damage. Similarly it was originally held that "a person saying to his agent, go forth and kill

---

[1] See *infra*, p. 104.

[2] On equity *vis-a-vis* law see : M. Eschelbacher, in Hermann Cohen Festschrift, Berlin 1912, 501-14; M. Güdemann, MGWJ LXI (1917) 422-43; Cohen, JRL, 49 ff.; M. Silberg, Law and Morals in the Talmudic Law (Hebrew), Jerusalem 1952; M. Silberg, Principia Talmudica (Hebrew), Jerusalem 1962, 97-138. As to the code of Hasidim : Finkelstein, Pharisees, LXXVIII-XC; S.B. Hoenig, JQR LVI (1965-6) 346 f., and B. de Vries Memorial Volume (Hebrew), Jerusalem 1968, 62-69; I. Baer, Israel among the Nations (Hebrew); I. Baer, Zion (Hebrew) XVII (1951/2), 1-55, XXVII (1961/2) 117-155; S. Safrai, JJS XVI (1965), 15-33. As to equity in Greek Law, Jones, Law, 64 ff.

a certain person, the agent is liable and his principal is not", until Shammai the Elder instructed, apparently at the trial of young Herod,[1] "and his principal is liable", apparently meaning "liable by the *laws of Heaven*" (TB Qiddushin 43a).

The law of Heaven was invoked mainly to render liable in tort a person who had created "*a mere cause*" (i.e. indirect injury) (T Baba Kama VI 16-17; Shebu'oth III 1-3; TB Gittin 53a, Qiddushin 24b). The same rule applies where goods were abandoned in a public place and afterwards caused harm : "If his pitcher broke and he did not remove it, or his camel fell and he did not cause it to stand up—he is not liable by laws of men, but is liable by the *laws of Heaven*".Later on R. Meir held that the liability was by the laws of men as well (M Baba Kama III 1, TB Baba Kama 28 b), just as he was in favour of liability in cases of remote cause (TB Baba Kama 100a).

The idea of *within the line of law* is similar. Law, *din*, in this context, denotes the boundary between neighbours, and the meaning of the idiom is that a person should not make use of the land up to the very boundary line but should remain well within his own property. The contrary case is where a person oversteps the law against his fellow-man (M Middoth II 2), in other words where he moves back the landmark between him and his neighbour.[2]

It appears that the Pietists (*Ḥasidim*) who organized themselves in groups during the Hasmonean period, took upon themselves special rules of halakha beyond the general halakha. Everyone joining the group "practices the quality of piety", as recounted in "*the laws of the pious*" (Aboth de- R. Nathan A 12; B 27).

Many of these special rules dealt with matters of tort, and their echo is heard in the words of R. Judah : "A person who wishes to be a *ḥasid* should observe matters of *tort*" (TB Baba Kama 30a). We are told of classes of commandments the observance of which was required of a person wishing to be accepted as an *associate* or a *trusted person* and there was probably a code of torts to which a *ḥasid* was similarly expected to submit himself. Perhaps the wording of M Baba Kama I 2, in the first person, is derived from a formula of such submission : the declarant undertakes to observe not only the obligations in tort set forth in the Torah but also those arising from other forms of

---

[1] See Schalit, Herod 31-33.

[2] To "*divert justice*" has a similar meaning, derived from diverting the boundary of a person at the expense of his neighbour. For "let the law penetrate the mountain" see *supra*.

pecuniary damage, and not only where he facilitated all the damage but also if there was an additional cause which contributed to the damage. Such an undertaking befits a code of *ḥasidim*.

A number of other rules from such a code are worthy of mention.[1] Generally a person walking in a public thoroughfare who injures somebody is not liable, but Issai b. Judah,[2] contrary to the opinion of another scholar, extends the liability. According to him, if two were proceeding in a public thoroughfare, one walking and the other running, and the latter injured the former, he is liable (TB Baba Kama 32a). The Pietists also extended the doctrine of vicarious liability : "It was said of R. Jose the Priest, and some say it was said of R. Jose the Pious, that nothing written by him was ever found in the hands of a Gentile" (TB Shabbath 19a).[3] The pietist was afraid to entrust a letter to a Gentile, lest he carry it on the Shabbath, and as a result the pietist would be causing the Gentile to work for him. The Shabbath, moreover, was too sanctified even in thought, and therefore it was a quality of piety that if the pietist only thought of a certain piece of work on the Shabbath he would not perform it even after the Shabbath was over (TB Shabbath 150 b).[4]

It is characteristic of a pietist not to consider an offence remedied until he is sure that what had to be done is done quite properly. Following the principle R. Akiba replied to "a pietist who had bought from one of two people and could not recall from which of them ... You have no remedy but to pay each of them" (TB Baba Kama 103b). Later on R. Akiba extended the doctrine to other matters : "There is no way to assure that she (a woman of non-priestly descent who testifies alone that her husband, a priest, died) does not commit a sin unless she is allowed neither to remarry nor to eat of the priestly offerings" (M Yebamoth XV 7).[5] This is characteristic of the caution which the pietists exercised and of the extent to which they endeavoured to keep away from sin.

---

[1] For the other rules see B. de Vries Memorial Volume, (Hebrew), 62.

[2] Identical with Yosse Qatnutha the Pious (M Sotah IX 15); Safrai, *ibid.*, 22, following TJ Baba Kama III 7, 3d. However see A. Goldberg, Kiryath Sefer XLV (1970) 327.

[3] Safrai, *ibid.* 21.

[4] Safrai, *ibid.* 21.

[5] Safrai, *ibid.* 22.

13. Right of Kings and Need of the Hour.

During the reigns of Jannaeus and Herod various acts were done not according to the Halakha of the Sages and despite their protest. Subsequent generations tried to bring these acts within an all-embracing system of Halakha, leaving no field of activity unregulated. Thus, the Halakha retreated when the Kings refused to argue their cases before the Sages; then the maxim was formulated : "The King never tries cases and is himself never tried" (M Sanhedrin II 2).[1]

It was likewise noted that the king put people to death not according to the modes of execution provided in the Torah. So it was said that "four modes of execution were provided for the Court, for secular authority only the sword was designated" (T Sanhedrin IX 10). This was the mode "used by *the regime*" (M Sanhedrin VII 3), and it was not considered untoward that the king of Israel should do as the Roman kings did.[2]

It is a fact that not everything that the king did met with the approval of the Sages; and outstanding example of their attitude is revealed in the matter of Herod's decree to sell the "robbers" abroad into slavery. The illegal intention in this case was quite apparent, and there was therefore no one who was ready to justify the king's decision.[3] But in less outstanding matters the Sages did not abide by their critical stand, and in the end they justified the decisions of the king. Later on the Exilarch met with the same reaction when he applied Persian law and not the law of the Torah (TB Baba Kama 58b).[4]

Another attempt to justify deviations from the halakha is the principle of the *need of the hour*. It was remembered that the Hasmonean

---

[1] Our assumption here is that the main point of this rule of halakha is that "the king is never tried", and in this connection it was further asserted that "the king never tries cases", and that this rule resulted from the trial of young Herod : TB Sanhedrin 19a; Josephus, Antiquities XIV, 9, 4, 171; Schalit, Herod, 33, 358. It is however possible that the main rule was that the king never tries cases and that it referred to certain acts of Herod who decided cases contrary to the view of the Sanhedrin, such as selling thieves to foreign slavery: Josephus, Antiquities, XVI, 1, 1, 1 ff.; Schalit, Herod 124, 418.

[2] See RQ 24 (1969) 569.

[3] Josephus, Antiquities XVI, 1, 1, 1-5; Schalit, Herod 126.

[4] As to the right of kings : Maimonides, Hilkhoth Melakhim III, 10; Hilkhoth Sanhedrin XVIII, 6. And see Tchernowitz, History IV, 225; I. Herzog, Talpioth (Hebrew) VII (1957/8), 4-32. The Exilarch may have wanted in this way to avert appeals to the Persian courts.

had sworn to fight the sinners (I Maccabees II 44, 48; III 5-6; VI 21; VII 23-24) and to punish the Hellenophiles (I Maccabees III 15; IV 2; VII 5, IX 25; XI 21-25). The war began by the killing of a Jew about to make a sacrifice to the Greek idol in Modiʻin (I Maccabees II 24). These were acts of war, not according to the rigour of the law, and only in later generations were they made part and parcel of halakha : "Any person who steals a holy jar or *curses by magic* or has intercourse with an Aramaean woman...—zealots may kill him" (M Sanhedrin IX 6).[1] Such punishment was eventually justified because they were *the need of the hour* (TJ Sanhedrin VI 9, 23c) or, in the words of R. Elizer b. Jacob. "According to my oral tradition the court may inflict corporal and other punishment not according to the Torah, yet not so as to contravene the words of the Torah but to make a fence for the Torah; and there was a case of a man who rode a horse on the Sabbath in the days of the Greeks and he was brought before the court and was stoned, not because he deserved it but because it was the need of the hour" (TB Sanhedrin 46a).[2]

Acts of zeal were common among the priests in the temple, and they were accorded recognition by the Sages : "If a priest functioned when impure, his fellow-priests would not bring him to the court, but the junior priests would take him out of the courtyard and kill him off with branches" (M Sanhedrin IX 6).[3] In a similar vein R. Eliezer b. Jacob again reports : "Once they found my mother's brother asleep, and they burnt his clothes". Accordingly a rule was laid down : "If he was clearly asleep, the officer in charge would beat him with his stick, and he had the right to burn his clothes. Then they would say, what is the noise in the courtyard ?—The noise of a Levite being beaten and his clothes being burnt for his having slept during his watch" (M Middoth I 2).

It may be that a number of rules in the Mishna belong to this category, without expressly being referred to as such. Originally they were deviations for the law of the Torah, but later they became pre-

---

[1] The right of the individual to punish criminals is mentioned also in the writings of Philo. See Alon, Studies I, 98-106; Cohen, JRL, 632 ff.

[2] R. Eliezer b. Jacob attributes the authority to the court and not to the Zealots. Compare the incident in which Shimon b. Shetaḥ hanged eighty witches on one day (M Sanhedrin VI 4).

[3] Cf. T. Kelim, Baba Kama I 6.

cedents for zealots or were justified as needs of the hour—and eventually they were accepted as halakha for all time.[1]

The law that every foreigner who draws nigh to the Temple is punishable with death is perhaps no more than a formulation based on the acts of zealots. This rule was inscribed, as we know, on a stone in the Temple walls, and the stone has been preserved to this very day.[2] The rule was first issued as a privilege granted by the Greek regime, but it was formulated upon the request of the Jews, and the request may have been submitted in accordance with a precedent created by the zealots.[3]

---

[1] As to zealotry see also M. Hengel, Die Zeloten, Leiden 1961, 152 ff.

[2] Cf. Josephus, War V, 194; VI, 125; Antiquities XV, 11, 5, 417; E. Bickerman, JQR XXXVII (1946-7) 387-405.

[3] Cf. TB Pesaḥim 3 b. See also A.M. Rabello, in Christian News from Israel XXI (1970) nos 3 and 4.

CHAPTER TWO

SECTARIAN HALAKHA

1. SAMARITANS

Since the days of the Second Temple there exists a parallel halakha to that of the Scribes and the Pharisees, namely, the halakha of the Samaritans.[1] The legal development of this community is unfolded by three sources.

First, there is a series of Aramaic bills from the end of the period of Persian rule (375-335 B.C.E.) which were taken from Samaria to a cave near Jericho and were found there. They include bills of sale of slaves and other bills which illustrates legal practices in the neighbourhood of Samaria. When this material is published it will be necessary to compare it to the Aramaic and Greek bills from Egypt, to the new Babylonian bills and to the Talmudical halakha, in order to determine the Samaritans' position and their attitude to more ancient traditions of the Israelites.[2]

The second source of information concerning the Samaritan halakha is their version of the Torah scroll. The Samaritan version is written in Western Hebrew script (*libuna'ah*), and it contains many variations and additions compared to our Massoratic text of the Torah. Certain passages may be explained as commentary, parallel to the Oral Law, and the version can serve to indicate the antiquity of a number of midrashim. Some of the additions have their parallels in the Septuagint and in the Aramaic translations, and there are even parallels in the Dead Sea scrolls. A number of examples of such *oral law* that was preserved in the *written law* of the Samaritans are worthy of note.[3]

---

[1] Regarding the Samaritans see J. Bowman, VT VII (1957) 184-9; *idem*, Bulletin of John Rylands Library XL (1958) 298-327; *idem*, Annual of Leeds University Oriental Society I (1959) 43-54; J. Mc Donald, BZAW 84 (1963); *idem*, The Theology of the Samaritans, London 1964 (including bibliography); J. Bowman, Samaritanische Probleme, Stuttgart 1967.

[2] It is a pity these bills have not yet been published : F.M. Cross, BA XXVI (1963) 110 ff.; *idem*, BASOR 175 (1964) 10; A.F. Rainey, PEQ IC (1967) 32-41.

[3] As to the Samaritan version of the Torah see H. Heller, The Samaritan Version of the Torah—a Copy from the Masoretic Version (Hebrew), Berlin 1924; M.Z. Segal, Introduction to the Bible (Hebrew), Jerusalem 1952, 911 ff.; S. Talmon, in Biblical Lexicon (Hebrew) 292-294 (including bibliography).

Ex. XVIII 20 : *Torah* instead of *toroth* (laws) in the plural, for at
the time the term *toroth* could not be understood to mean a number
of individual decisions but only a generic term for the written law.
Thus also the Aramaic translation of Onkelos, whereas the scholars
of Yabne considered *Toroth* to be individual provisions of halakha
(Mekhilta *ad loc.*).—Ex. XXI 4 : *La'adonaw* (his master's) instead of
la'adoneha (her master's) : for when the slave and the wife belong to
different masters the patriarchal principle operates, and the children
belong to the master of the slave. This variation is also to be found
in the Aramaic translations.—Ex. XXI 18 : the words "with a stone
or with his fist" are absent, so that no instrument of killing is excluded
(cf. Mekhilta *ad loc.*).—Ex XXII 4 (interpolation) : the word *yab'e*
instead of *yab'ir* (cause to be eaten), as in M Baba Kama 1. 1.[1]—Ex
XXII 8 : *Yarshi'enu* (he shall condemn him) instead of *yarshi'un*
(they shall condemn), for the use of the plural is a relic from the
language of idolaters and was rejected by the commentators.—Ex
XXIII, 4 : the words "or any beast of his" are inserted, so that the
commandment to return the loss be extended to include any beast.[2]

The existence of identical interpretations in the Samaritan Torah
and in the Torah of Sages shows that their source may lie in the Persian
period. In that ancient period there probably existed such relations
between Jews and Samaritans that facilitated the acceptance of
tradition from one another.[3]

The third source are books of halakha which, though written in
the middle ages, are based on a tradition which began in the days
of the Temple. The work *kitab al-kafi* describing the Samaritan
halakha, was written in the eleventh century in Arabic by Joseph b.
Solomon of the Shkhem area. A similar book is *Tabah*, meaning com-
pendium, written in the next century by Ibn al-Hasan al-Suri.[4] At

---

[1] The synonymous *ba'a* was apparently chosen to facilitate the memorizing of the
passages which both use the verb "*ba'ar*". Using a different key word was sufficient
to help the memory, but the Samaritans went as far as introducing the word into the
text itself.

[2] Many additional illustrations are furnished by Heller.

[3] Friendly relations actually existed even in the times of the Tannaim : T Pasha
II 3 (I 15); but after Alexander's conquest they apparently ceased to learn from each
other, as at that time, the Samaritan temple was erected : Josephus Antiquities XI 8, 2,
306 ff.; TB Yoma 69a; Megillath Ta'anith (Lichtenstein, HUCA VIII-IX 339).

[4] D. Abdel Al, A comparative Study of the inedited work of Abu 'l Hasan el Suri and
Jusuf ibn Salama, Diss, Leeds 1957.

that time Monia b. Sadga Abu al-Faraj, in *Kitab al-Ḥalaf*, counted the points upon which the Samaritans and the Jews differed.

The Samaritans recognize the sanctity of the Torah only, for they assign their secession from the tribe of Judah to the days of Eli the priest. The leadership of the community remained in the hands of the priests, who receive from the people tithes, the shoulder and the cheeks. The priests conduct the various ceremonies, such as circumcision, betrothal, divorce and burial. At the head of the community there stood a council (cf. Josephus, Antiquities XVIII, 4, 2, 88), which may have also represented the Samaritans who settled in distant cities.

The Sages admitted that "every commandment which the *Kuthim* (Samaritans) maintained they did so more meticulously than Israel" (T Pasḥa II 3 (I, 15)). Thus they were very particular in matters of consanguinity, and prohibited the marriage of a man to the daughter of his brother or of his sister. [1] They also prohibited bigamy except if the first wife was barren, and in no case did they allow the taking of a second or third wife. At the betrothals an instrument was drawn up, called *letter of clinging* which includes the husband's right to annul or ratify his wife's vows, and the obligation that "her food, her raiment, and her conjugal rights, shall he not diminish". The instrument also mentions the undertaking of the wife to obey and not disobey him and to be a help meet for him.[2]

2. HELLENIZERS

After the country was conquered by Alexander the Great the Jews remained entitled to live according to *the laws of their ancestors* or *the laws of the community of Jews*. The ruling power did not want to apply Greek law to the Jews, and preferred to allow them to continue to have their disputes settled before their own judges and according to their own laws. Strabon reports that the Jewish Ethnarch in Egypt "rules the people and decides on matters of law and supervises the contracts and statutes as if he were a ruler of an independent state" (Josephus, Antiquities XIV, 7, 2, 117). Thus the Jewish court dealt with civil matters, and attached to it there was a special archive for bills.

---

[1] The Pharisees, on the other hand, stressed the praiseworthiness of such marriage : T Qiddushin I 4; TB Yebamoth 62b. Cf. Tarbiz (Hebrew) XXXII (1962/63) 19ff., the article on marriage in the Biblical Encyclopedia (Hebrew); Rabin, QS 91 ff.

[2] M. Gaster MGWJ LIV (1910) 181 ; cf. JJS VIII (1957) 215-7.

Similar autonomy was granted to the Jews in Asia Minor (Josephus, Antiquities XIV, 10, 17, 235) and no doubt to their brethren in Palestine as well.[1]

However, despite such judicial autonomy, many Greek concepts penetrated Jewish thought and left their imprint on halakha and law as well. The Greek terms mentioned in the Mishna and the Talmud testify to this;[2] they probably became current in halakha before the Hasmonean reaction against Greek culture.[3] The same assumption applies to other rules of halakha for which there is no authority in the Torah, and have their parallels in Greek sources. It may be reasonably assumed that at least some of these parallels indicate a cultural assimilation of Jews in the culture of the Ptolemaic or Seleucid rulers.[4]

In between Talmudic halakha and Greek law special space must be reserved for various commentaries on the Torah, as preserved in the Septuagint and in the words of Philo of Alexandria on the special laws. There are some who wished to find in deviations from the oral law an independent tradition of the Jews of Egypt.[5] Others, on the contrary, stressed the compatibility of Philo with the ancient halakha, as distinct from the halakha in its final form.[6] In any case, if such an independent halakha of the Jews of Egypt did exist, its growth was due to a clash between circumstances of life and laws not easily changed such as family law.[7]

---

[1] H.J. Wolff, RIDA[3] VII (1960) 215. On the other hand see V. Tcherikover, CPJ I, 32 ff., 238, and see L.H. Feldman, Jew. Social Studies XXII (1960) 215-237; J. Modrzejewski, Iura XII, (1961) 162 ff.

[2] See S. Kraus, Griechische und lateinische Lehnwörter im Talmud, Midrash und Targum, Berlin 1898-9.

[3] Afterwards, though the rulers became hellenized, the rabbis probably rejected Greek influence beyond that already established.

[4] Zacharia Frankel wrote about this influence, and he was followed by L. Blau, MGWJ LXIII (1919) 138 ff., Gulak, Urkundenwesen; Ostersetzer, Haṣofé le—Hokhmath Israel (Hebrew), 1936, 185-194; A. Tcherikover, The Jews in Egypt (Hebrew), ch. IV; Lieberman, Greek; id, Hellenism; 1. Baer, Zion (Hebrew) 17 (1952) and (1962). See also Cohen, JRL 24. 756, 760, who refers to further sources.

[5] E.R. Goodenough, The Jurisprudence of the Jewish Courts in Egypt, New Haven 1929.

[6] Belkin, Philo; and Alon, Studies, I 83-114.

[7] Examples of this are the reforms which enable the cancellation of betrothals without a bill of divorcement : Falk, JML 46 ff.

3. SADDUCEES

Megillath Ta'anith counts among the days on which fasting is not permitted, the 4th of Tammuz, on which "the *Book of Decrees* was found", apparently referring to a book of laws used by the Sanhedrin when the Sadducees were the dominant force in it.[1] If we do not wish to rely on the medieval scholium, we have little knowledge regarding the differences between the halakha of the Sadducees and that of the Pharisees. The main difference was that the Sadducees rejected *the oral law* or *words of the Scribes*, holding instead that the "Torah is bound up and laid down and anyone who wishes to may come and learn (TB Qiddushin 66a),[2] or, the way Josephus puts it (Antiquities XIII 1, 6, 298): "Only written laws should be considered as such, whereas those derived from *ancestral tradition* need not be kept".

Due to their strict adherence to the expression of scripture the Sadducees apparently rejected a number of interpretations which tended to leniency in penalties, as Josephus relates (*ibid.*) "that the Pharisees are by their nature lenient in penal law" (and see M Makkoth I 10). The Sadducees, further, rejected the Pharisee halakha that "false witnesses are not to be put to death unless the case has been decided", holding instead that "false witnesses are not to be put to death unless (the accused man) has been executed" (M Makkoth I 6). The intent of the Pharisees may originally have been that malicious witnesses may be put to death only between the decision of the case and the execution of the accused, this being a short time, since justice should never be delayed. The Sadducees, on the other hand, held that the rule concerning malicious witnesses takes effect only after the accused has been executed—but thenceforth its effect was unlimited. If this is a right construction of the argument, it confirms the accepted view that the Pharisees were lenient and the Sadducees strict in their legal approach.[3]

---

[1] Regarding the Sadducees see A. Geiger, Collection of Essays (Hebrew); R. Leszynsky, Die Sadduzäer, Berlin, 1912; J. Wellhausen, Die Pharisäer und die Sadducäer, Hannover 1924; R.T. Herford, The Pharisees, London 1924; W. Beilner, BZ N.F. III (1959) 235-51; S. Zeitlin, JQR LII (1961-62) 97-139; Finkelstein, Pharisees; A. Michel and J. Le Moyne, Dictionnaire de la Bible, Suppl. VII (1966) s.v. *Pharisees;* R. Meyer, Tradition und Neuschöpfung im Antiken Judentum, Berlin 1965; V. Eppstein, JBL LXXXV (1966), 213-24.

[2] This resembles the words of Anan ben David : Seek well in the Torah and do not rely on my opion.

[3] Cf. Finkelstein, Pharisees, 144, 696, 899.

Generally the Sadducees relied only on Scripture, yet they recognized certain extensions of the law by way of analogy and *a fortiori* reasoning. Their doctrine of vicarious liability in tort must be viewed in this light (M Yadayim IV 7) : even if the reasoning set forth ascribed to the Sadducees dates from after the Destruction, the tradition with regard to the rule of halakha itself is reliable, and it obviously proceeds upon analogy removed from the letter of the law. The Pharisees did not object to the reasoning of the Sadducees in this matter, and the objections which they did raise and which were decisive were of a utilitarian nature (*ibid.*).[1]

According to the Sadducees the daughter and the son's daughter take share and share alike, whereas the Pharisees stood for the doctrine of *representation* which has no foundation in the Torah and hence held that the whole estate went to the son's daughter (TB Baba Bathra 115b; T Yadayim II 20; TJ Baba Bathra VIII 1, 16a).[2] The principle of representation was established by the Scribes, and the Sadducees did not recognize that it could operate in derogation of the daughter's rights.

The scholium of Megillath Ta'anith ascribes to the Sadducees the idea of *an eye for an eye—literally*, but this opinion could be found among the Pharisees (TB Baba Kama 84a; Josephus, Antiquities IV 8.35.280).[3] The scholium also ascribes to the Sadducees the opinion that "spreading the garment", in the case of the "bringer of an evil name" (Deut. XXII, 14, 17), is to be taken literally; this interpretation is also accepted by some of the Sages (Sifre Deut. 235-237). Again, in the case of loosening the shoe, that the woman should literally spit in the face of her husband's brother (Deut. XXV 9) is an interpretation which was not limited to the school of the Sadducees.[4]

There is however a doubt as to whether the views of the Sadducees were ever put into practice, even when they dominated the Sanhedrin. Josephus (Antiquities XVIII 1, 4, 17) says that "they do nothing (according to their own view) if it can (so) be said. For when they attain power they unwillingly and even perforce, act according to the doctrines of the Pharisee, as otherwise they would not be tolerated by the masses". This may be the reason why information as to their laws is so scant.

---

[1] Finkelstein, 283 f., 698 f.

[2] Finkelstein, 138 ff., 694 ff.

[3] Finkelstein, 720, 815.

[4] See Albeck, Mishna, Introduction to Tractate Yebamoth.

4. Essenes and the Dead Sea Community

Both Philo of Alexandria and Josephus [1] devote space in their books to a description of the way of life of the Essenes [2], and this description furnishes an idea of their views on legal matters. The Essenes were organized as a society whose purpose was to serve the Lord; thus they carry on the tradition of the original pietists and resemble the Pharisee grouping. Viewed from another angle, the organisation of the Essenes resembles that of parallel bodies in Greece and in Egypt. [3]

All in all, according to Josephus, the Essenes counted about four thousand members, living outside Jerusalem and the other cities. Joining the group entailed a protracted and difficult procedure, in which the sincerity of the candidate was tested. At the end of the trial period the candidate swore to submit in full to the laws of the sect. Even after joining, the new member remained subject to planned gradual progress as the group was organized by classes according to seniority and age, every person being obliged to realize where he belongs and to obey the orders of the leading members. [4]

Despite strict discipline and hierarchal management, the group's organisation was democratic in form. The *supervisor* appointed for entertaining guests, and apparently for other duties as well, was elected by popular vote, perhaps for a definite period. [5] Judicial authority was also, apparently, vested in the group as a whole, "and they would not sit in judgment if their number was less than a hundred men". On other occasions a *quorum* of ten was required to begin, and "no one open his mouth unless the nine consent". [6] There was, no doubt, a set of penalties for offenders, the most severe punishment being outright expulsion from the group. [7]

Community of property was a basic principle, and the resulting communal life brought the members together for meals and other

---

[1] Philo, Quod omnis probis; Apologia; Josephus, War II 8; Antiquities XI 1. 11 ff.

[2] Regarding the Essenes see : I. Baer, Israel among the Nations (Hebrew) Jerusalem, 1955, 18 ff.; S. Wagner, Die Essener in der wissensch. Diskussion, BZAW 79 (1960) 284 f.

[3] E. Seidl, PtRG, 152 ff.

[4] Josephus, War II 8.6, 7, 10.

[5] Josephus, War II 8.4.

[6] Josephus, War II 8.9.

[7] Josephus, War II 8.8.

occasions. The very substance of the grouping was its partnership (*koinonia*),[1] from which there grew its objection to all dealings in property.[2] Most of the Essenes objected to marriage, and to women in general,[3] but some of them did not go so far but remained very particular about selecting their wives and in their marital relations.[4] Egalitarian sentiments brought them to oppose slavery,[5] and due both to their pietism and their strict adherence to the truth they forbade all oaths.[6]

Resembling the Essenes were the Dead Sea Community and the congregation of the *Damascus Covenant*. In these, again, the candidate had to pass a preparatory period, and would progress by grades.[7] At the head of the Community there stood the *Head Officer*,[8] the *Controller* [9] and the *Community Council*, composed of priests and others.[10] Supreme authority rested with the *public*, the general meeting of the Community, which decided on the laws of the Community and elected the leaders. Part of the Manual of Discipline is therefore devoted to the general meeting and its procedure.[11]

A set of rules was set forth in the *Manual of Discipline* and in the *Damascus Covenant*, and the candidate for membership must subject himself to them and swear to keep them.[12] Following the hierarchal structure of the sect every member is graded also by age, until he attains full rights and duties;[13] his fitness for his standing is tested annually by renewal of the covenant and the oath.[14]

A number of offences were recorded in a book, as laid down by the public and as determined by the judges or the general assem-

---

[1] Philo, Quod omnis, 86; Apologia XI, 1, 4, 5; Josephus, War II 8.3; Antiquities XVIII 1.5.20;

[2] Josephus, War II 8.4.

[3] Josephus, War II 8.2; Antiquities XVIII 1.5.21; Philo, Apologia 11, 14.

[4] Josephus, War II 8.13.

[5] Jospehus, Antiquities XVIII, 1, 5, 21; Philo, Quod omnis, 79.

[6] Josephus, War II 8.6. Philo Quod omnis 84.

[7] Manual of Discipline (MD) V 20-25, VI 13-23; and see S. Lieberman, JBL LXXI (1952) 199 ff.; Rabin, QS 1-21.

[8] MD VI 14.

[9] MD VI 12, 20; Damascus Covenant (DC) XIII 7-19.

[10] MD VI 18; VIII 1-4.

[11] MD VI 8-13.

[12] MD I 1-15; DC VI 12 — VII 4.

[13] MD A 6-17.

[14] MD I 16-25, V, 20-22.

bly [1]. Upon these laws becoming operative, rules of evidence also became stricter, and especially all offenders were disqualified to testify.[2]

Since the members of the Community left Jerusalem in order to settle in the wilderness, they too, like the Essenes, led a communal life, although private property among them is recorded.[3] Members of the sect were strongly opposed to polygamy and to marrying nieces,[4] but did not refrain from matrimony.

Notwithstanding the external difference between the rules of the Essenes and those of the Community, their laws resemble each other and the halakha of the Pharisees, and especially the concepts that were apparently accepted by the pietists and associates.[5]

5. CHRISTIANS

The small Judaeo-Christian sect at the end of the Second Commonwealth apparently followed the halakha generally accepted.[6] However they held reservations as to certain laws; in part they followed the opinions of previous sects, in part their reservations reveal the influence of the European world, which reached them through Christians of other nations, and some reservations represent the personal opinions of their leaders.

Under the influence of the Essenes, the attitude of the Christians to marital relations, to marriage and to worldly affairs in general, was equivocal and at times negative. On the one hand abstinence was not required of all believers, as the apostleship and conversion had to go on, but abstinence was considered fitting for everyone devoting himself to the service of Christ, and in the kingdom of heaven it would prevail.[7]

---

[1] MD VI 24-VII 25, VIII 16-IX 2; DC IX 1-22.

[2] DC IX 20-X 3. Disqualifications for testimony were apparently created, however, more as a penalty for offenders than as halakha concerning rules of evidence.

[3] Rabin, QS 22-36.

[4] DC IV 19-V 11; Rabin, op. cit., 91 ff.

[5] This matter has been well explained in Rabin's work. Regarding the halakha of the sect see also J. Licht, The Manual of Discipline (Hebrew), Jerusalem, 1965; H.S. Siedl, Qumran, Eine Mönchsgemeinde in Alten Bund, Roma 1963; C.H. Hunziger, in H. Bardtke, Qumran Probleme, Berlin 1963, 231-47; G.R. Driver, The Judaean Scrolls Oxford 1965, and the periodical Revue de Qumran.

[6] Regarding modern literature dealing with legal matters in the gospels, see Cohen, JRL, XVI, 757 f.

[7] Matthew XIX, 12, XXII 30, Luke XIV 26.

On the other hand, for the present and for the wider group, the prohibition of bigamy was accepted and divorce was rejected.[1] Monogamy was the general practice of the Christians from the cultural spheres of Greece and Rome, and quite understandably they showed their co-religionists what the defects of polygamy were. The position of the Christians may also be considered to reflect an attitude giving women equality with men, and such an attitude is incompatible with the patriarchal regime of matrimony accepted in the Halakha. The Essenes already regarded all men as equal, and therefore rejected slavery; their opinions may have been extended among the Christians to apply to women as well. However there also existed other opinions among the Christians.[2]

This approach may also have been a determinant factor regarding inheritance laws. The disciples of Jesus, like the Essenes, had little regard for worldly objects, and apparently did not consider the laws of succession important.[3] However, with the passage of time there arose among some of them a critical attitude towards the patriarchal character of the Halakha. In the church, said Paul, "there is neither Jew nor Greek, there is neither bond nor free, there is neither male nor female".[4] Hence certain Christians whose cultural origins were western, held that men and women should be made equal for all legal purposes,[5] including laws of inheritance, and thus "the son and the daughter shall inherit alike".[6] This was not generally accepted. Some of them maintained the rule of halakha that "where there is a son the daughter shall not inherit"—and thus the individual decider remained free to choose which opinion to follow.

The early Christians claimed that Christ did not come to destroy the law or the prophets : "I have only come *to add to the law of Moses*,[7] meaning that the demand of Christianity was in the nature of *heavenly law*, beyond the strict letter of the law. At a later stage, in the course of dispute with the Sages, another argument was adduced, that the

---

[1] Matthew V 31, XIX 3-9; Mark X 2; Luke XVI 18; and see Falk, JML 19 ff., 66 ff., 132 ff.

[2] For instance, Paul's view that women should be silent in public, I Corinthians XIV 34.

[3] Cf. Luke XII 14.

[4] Galatians III 28; cf. in Tana d'Be Eliyahu Rabba IX (X), passage beginning "and Deborah".

[5] See Mekhilta of R. Simon b. Yoḥai, beginning of Mishpatim (Epstein-Melamed 158).

[6] TB Shabbath 116 b. This is a quotation from an Aramaic gospel; see Tarbiz (Hebrew) XXIII, (1952) 9-15.

[7] Matthew V 17; TB Shabbath 116b.

Torah only permitted certain things because of evil inclinations ("the hardness of heart", *sclerokardia*).[1] Still later on, the words of Jesus were given precedence over those of the Torah, and they were interpreted as repealing some of the commandments or even all of them.[2]

---

[1] Matthew XIX 8; cf. TB Qiddushin 21 b.
[2] John V 17 and Epistles of Paul in many places.

CHAPTER THREE

CONSTITUTION

1. POLITICAL FRAMEWORK

Persian policy was fair to the nations in the countries of the Empire, and allowed each nation *to use its own language* and preserve the rites of its ancestors. Moreover, the Achaimeni kings wanted to be recognized as rulers of a country according to the rites of the gods of that country.[1] Hence the decree of Cyrus that the Temple at Jerusalem be built at his expense, and hence the privileged position of the clergy who were exempted from state taxes. The returning exiles in Jerusalem and in the rest of the country were allowed to act as a political community enjoying autonomy not only in matters of religion and worship but also in matters of law and administration. This is evidenced by coins with the Hebrew inscription *Yehud*,[2] by the right to build a wall around Jerusalem, by Jewish judges entitled to try cases and by giving effect to the laws of the Torah.

Judea belonged to the area governed by the satrap of *Abar Nahara*, which apparently was the state of *Athora* (Syria). At the head of the land of Judea there stood a governor, Persian or Jewish, who was appointed by the Persian ruling power and under him, and apparently appointed by him, there functioned the heads of districts or deputies. [3] Judges were attached to each satrap to administer the laws of the kingdom and to supervise the work of the local judges (Ezra IV 9),[4] who in turn were supposed to administer *the law of thy God and the law of the king* (Ezra VII 26); in other words, the law of Israel applied to the extent that it was not modified by Persian legislation. This was in

---

[1] A. Christensen, Die Iranier (Handbuch d. Altertumswissenschaft) (-3.1), München 1933, 253; Zucker, Studien 16 f.

[2] As to these coins and who struck them see Tcherikover, Hellenistic, 417 n. 2.

[3] For the administrative division of the empire see Lehmann-Haupt, RE II 3 (1921) *s.v. Satrap;* P.J. Junge, Klio XXXIV (1941) 1-55, and for the names of the imperial officials : W. Eilers, Iranische Beamtennamen, Abhandlungen d. deutschen Gesellschaft f.d. Kunde des Morgenlandes, XXV, 5 (1940); Zucker, Studien, 21.

[4] See also Cowley, AP 1[3], 6[6], 16[3], [7], and Ed. Meyer, Geschichte des Altertums IV[2], 1, 60 f.; Zucker, 12 ff.: A. Christensen, Die Iranier, 272 ff.

accordance with Persian policy, to utilise the legal tradition of the various nations.[1]

When Alexander the Great passed through Palestine, the High Priest and the Elders appeared before him and requested him to confirm Jewish autonomy. Alexander apparently granted their request, allowed control to remain in the hands of the High Priest, and confirmed the right of the Jews *to live according to the laws of their ancestors*.[2] At or about his time the function of governor was allowed to expire, and instead all political power was vested in the High Priest. Although other states, such as Syria and Sidon, were ruled by a *strategos*, no such ruler was appointed for Judea.[3] The powers that were generally vested in these representatives were apparently vested in the High Priest, and he was also responsible for the payment of taxes. Although certain officials were subsequently appointed by the Ptolemaic regime, the king availed himself of the services of local Jews such as Tobias and his son Joseph. Such people were under the influence of Hellenistic culture, but the large majority of the people did not know Greek and continued to be governed by the laws of the Torah and tradition.

Even Antiochus III confirmed Jewish autonomy and the right to live *according to ancestral law;* he also exempted the Jews from certain taxes (Josephus, Antiquities XII, 3.3.138). But in 175 B.C.E. the Hellenistic party in Jerusalem gathered strength and succeeded "to register the people of Jerusalem as *people of Antioch*".[4] According to their plan there should be established in Jerusalem an Hellenistic polis, and Greek law should be applied to its inhabitants. As Antiochus was considered the founder and protector of the new city, worship in his honour was introduced, and following the accepted practice in Greek cities, the inhabitants could change the laws of the Torah and enact new laws in their stead.

The Hasmoneans restored the Torah to its status as the laws of the land, asserted the independence of Judea and annexed to it the re-

---

[1] Diodorus I 95; Ed. Meyer, Kleine Schriften II, Halle 1924, 94 ff.; A.F. Olmstead, American Journal of Semitic Languages LI (1935) 247 ff.; E. Bresciani, Studi Classici e Orientali VII (1958) 153 ff.; Falk, HL, 54 f.

[2] See Josephus, Antiquities XI 8. 304 ff.; Megillath Ta'anith; TB Yoma 69a; Tcherikover, Hellenistic, 41 ff.

[3] Tcherikover, Hellenistic 61 ff.; as to the function of the *strategos* see H. Bengtson, Die Strategie in der hellenistischen Zeit, MB 32, München 1944.

[4] II Maccabees IV 9; Tcherikover, Hellenistic, 161 ff. According to the parallel wording in Josephus, Antiquities XII 5.1.240, the Hellenizers wished to "maintain the Hellenic form of rule". See also V. Tcherikover, IEJ XIV (1964) 61-78.

maining parts of historical Israel. The Hasmonean High Priest was
first appointed as a representative of the Seleucid rule, but complete
independence was attained in the time of Simon the Hasmonean in
140 B.C.E., he being elected political, religious and military head.[1]

After seventy years of autonomous rule Pompey was presented with
a demand to cancel the rights of the Hasmonean brothers engaged in
strife and to restore theocracy under Roman rule : "The people asked
not to be subjected to the rule of kings, (saying) that by ancestral
tradition they are to obey the priests of the God whom they worship,
and that these (two), although of priestly descent, wish to carry the
people over to a different rule so that they should be slaves (to them)".[2]
Political independence was then abolished, although the High Priest
was authorised to serve as *prostates tou etnou*, head of the people, on
behalf of the Roman government. This authority included judicial
autonomy, but not the power to strike coins; this power and the
royal crown were given to Herod. After the death of Herod limited
autonomy was restored to the High Priest, who acted in political
matters and perhaps also in matters of capital offences, under the
supervision of the Roman provincial governor or of the king enthroned
by the Romans. Complete autonomy returned only for the short
period of the last rebellion and the war of the Destruction.[3]

2. The Great Synagogue

When the returning exiles comprised no more than a few thousand
people and lived in Jerusalem and in its immediate vicinity, it was
possible to discuss and decide matters in an assembly of family heads.
Such an assembly was apparently called *the great synagogue*,[4] and it
convened irregularly as the needs of the time required. Ezra's action
against the foreign women took place at an assembly of the people.
"And they made proclamation throughout Judah and Jerusalem unto
all the children of the captivity, that they should gather themselves
together unto Jerusalem; and that whosoever came not within three

---

[1] I Maccabees XIV 27-49; Tcherikover, Hellenistic, 239

[2] Josephus, Antiquities XIV 3.2.41; Zucker, Studien 50.

[3] As to this : C. Roth, JSS IX (1964) 295-319.

[4] With regard to the Great Synagogue see : E.A. Finkelstein, The Pharisees and the
Men of the Great Synagogue (Hebrew), New York 1950; Alon, History II 223; E. Bickerman, RB LIX (1952) 48; Honig, Sanh. 169; H. Mantel, HTR LX (1967) 69 ff. With
regard to public assemblies in general : Brandis, RE X, 2163-2220.

days, according to the counsel of the princes and the elders, all his
substance should be forfeited, and himself separated from the congregation of the captivity" (Ezra X 7-8)

The assembly was called at three days' notice by decision of the
princes and elders, who will be discussed further on. The proclamation
circulated among the people was apparently by crier who went out
to the cities of Judea and threatened potential absentees with the
penalties mentioned. After Ezra's words of reproach the people were
called upon to express their agreement : "Then all the congregation
answered and said with a loud voice : 'As thou hast said, so it is for us
to do' ..." (*ibid.* 12).

A similar assembly was apparently convened to decide upon the
matters included in the covenant (Neh X 1-40). The chapter consists
of minutes of an assembly, signed by eighty-four persons, "our princes,
our Levites, and our priests" (*ibid.* 1). But the signatories also represent the other participants in the gathering : "And the rest of the
people, the priests, the Levites, the porters, the singers the Nethinim,
and all they that separated themselves from the peoples of the lands
unto the law of God, their wives, their sons, and their daughters,
everyone that had knowledge and understanding" (*ibid.* 29). These
persons participated in the assembly and were mentioned in the
covenant, but did not themselves sign. This assembly decided to enact
statutes : "Also we made ordinances for us" (*ibid.* 33), in addition to
the Torah already long accepted. It is probable that the rest of the
decrees and statutes adapted by the men of *the great synagogue* (M
Aboth I 1, TJ Shekalim V 1, 48c) were brought before a similar assembly and adapted as a decision of the people.

In like fashion Joseph the son of Tobias, in 240 B.C.E., called the
people to an assembly in the Temple enclosure so as to receive full
powers for negotiations with the Ptolemaic authorities (Josephus,
Antiquities XII 4.2.164). On this occasion the initiator of the assembly
presided, presented the motions and declared the adoption of the
resolutions.

The affairs of the communities in Egypt were also frequently brought
before the whole membership. After the Septuagint was completed,
the Jews of Alexandria gathered to discuss future use of the translation and to prohibit any modification or addition (Epistle of Aristeas
310 ff.; Josephus, Antiquities XII 2.12.108).

Details of the functioning of the general meeting in the Hellenistic
period may be gathered from Ecclesiasticus. The community ap-

parently did not convene for extraordinary reasons only but rather
on set assembly days (cf. M Megillah I 1). The place of the assembly
was in the town square or near the gate, and it was therefore called
the gate gathering (Ecclesiasticus VII 7; XLII 11). Members of the
assembly dealt both with public affairs and theoretical study and
at times also tried offenders. Thus it is said of the adultress : "She
shall be led into the *assembly* (Ecclesiasticus XXIII 24; cf. *ibid.*
XLII 11, Ezekiel XVI 40, and the story of Susanna in the Septuagint). The members of the community also would remove a judge who
diverted justice, and apparently elected judges for fixed periods
(Ecclesiasticus VII 7). Although the assembly was open to all members, it was held that "the utterance of the prudent is sought for in
the assembly" (*ibid.* XXI 17), that is to say that the floor ws generally
held by the sages and the elders.

During the Maccabean wars the fighters took over the powers of
the community as a whole, but after the victory these powers were
restored, and therefore Simon was elected "in a great congregation
(*synagoge megale*) of priests and people and princes of the nation, and
of the elders of the country (I Maccabees XIV 28), and the message
of the Spartans was read out "before the *community* in Jerusalem"
(*ibid.* 19). Among the powers given to Simon presiding at the assembly
is mentioned : "and that it should not be lawful for anyone among the
people or among the priests to set at nought any of these things, or to
gainsay the things spoken by him, or to gather an *assembly* in the
country without him" (*ibid.* 44). The assembly may be meant by the
expression *corporation of the Jews* found on coins and in international
correspondence, functioning together with the High Priests or the
kings. Although Herod made no mention of such a *corporation* on his
coins, he frequently convened popular assemblies (Josephus, Antiquities XVI 4.6.132; XVI 11.7.393). [1] As to the trial of the accused
before the assembly (Josephus, Wars I 27.6.550; I 33.3.654), the king
may have followed Roman procedure. [2]

The tradition of the general assembly was preserved by the Essenes,
who according to Josephus (War II 8.9.145) "would not sit in judgment if their number was less than a hundred men." Detailed regulations for these meetings were laid down in the *Manual of Discipline*
of the Dead Sea group. *Public session* was held at fixed intervals, so

---

[1] Cf. Schalit, Herod, 154 ff.

[2] Lex XII tab. IX 2; Cicero, de leg. III 4, 11, but see Zucker, Studien 72.

as to enact statutes and to decide on public affairs, such as taxes for the treasury, admission of members and trial of offenders. There was a fixed order for seating, for granting the floor and for counting the votes, and decisions were adopted by a majority.[1]

Similar arrangements are mentioned in the halakha concerning the 23-member Sanhedrin : "The Sanhedrin sat in the form of half a circular threshing-floor, so that they might see each other, ... and three rows of scholars would sit in front of them, each one knowing his own place" (M Sanhedrin IV 3-4). "Further on, protocol ceased to apply, and anyone managing to procede the others into the four-cubit limit won his place" (T Sanhedrin VIII 2). This is a description of a large assembly convening in each of the cities of Israel, in order to try capital offences and to deal with public affairs and study the Torah. The Sanhedrin was nothing other than the community itself (cf. M Sanhedrin I 6), with the right of speech reserved to the ordained sages.

This session may have been called *society of the town* (e.g. M Berakhoth IV 7 ; T Megilla III 29), and the individuals were called *townsmen* or "members of the town".[2] But in the course of time the framework became more restricted and the *society* included only the *prominent people of the town* just as the Sanhedrin included only the sages. This, apparently, was part of the process in which the local democratic authorities were replaced by authorities appointed by the sages and by the prince.

3. The Elders

The Elders were at the head of the people during the Second Commonwealth as well as during the First. Ezra X 8 mentions the *counsel of the princes and the elders* before the general meeting. This title was later on preserved in the Mishna as *elders of Israel* (M Para III 7) or as *elders of court* (M Yoma I 3),[3] the former stressing representation of the people, the latter conceiving the elders as a body in its own right. The Aramaic term is *sabei Yehudaia* (elders of the Jews; Ezra VI 7 ff.), and it is possible that the nobles and rulers mentioned in Nehemia and

---

[1] Rabin, QS, 102 ff.

[2] As to this meaning of *Corporation of the town* cf. Lieberman, Tos. Kif. I 190, V, 1210; and see also Honig, JQR XLVIII (1957-58) 123; S. Safrai, Tarbiz (Hebrew) XXXV (1966) 313.

[3] As to the Elders see e.g. G. Bornkamm, Theologisches Wörterbuch zum Neuen Testament, VI 651 ff., *s.v. presbys*, and the bibliography indicated there.

the Jewish nobles mentioned in the Aramaic papyri in Elephantine [1]
are the same elders.

The Greek name for the council of elders, *gerousia*, first appears
in the Book of Judith. This book tells of the Persian era and it was
apparently translated in the third century B.C.E. by the translators
of the Septuagint. According to the account in Judith IV 8, XI 14 and
XV 8, the congregation of the Jews was led by the *council of elders*.[2]

Although the High Priest functioned under the Persian governor
and was in turn assisted by the heads of the priestly families, the
Persian regime recognized only the governor and the elders of the
Jews as a whole. Darius granted permission to build the Temple to
"the governor of the Jews and the *elders of the Jews*" (Ezra VI 7), or,
according to the Greek version of Ezra in the Septuagint, to "Zerubabel
the *hyparchus* of the Jews and the *elders of the Jews*".

In 410 B.C.E. the Jews of Elephantine wrote to the Jews in Palestine
to ask for help, and their letter was addressed to the governor and
"Joḥanan the High Priest and his colleagues the priests who are in
Jerusalem and to Ostanes the brother of Anani and the *nobles of the
Jews*".[3] Thus it appears that the letter was directed to the Persian
governor and to the Jewish leadership as well, the latter comprising
two institutions. On the one hand there stood the High Priest and
the corps of priests, and on the other—another person at the head of
the elders. It is possible that the appointment of a special person
to head the elders came about after the Persians no longer appointed
Jews as governors of Judea. If they did not want to leave all the
representation in the hands of the High Priest, they had to appoint
a separate head of the elders.

Yet towards the end of the Persian rule the High Priest gained
strength, although the double nature of the leadership was still noticeable. In the Book of Judith we notice that operating together there
were "the High Priest and the *gerousia* of all Israel sitting in Jerusalem"
(IV 8, XV 8); stressing that they no longer sat separately, but that
the council was composed of priests, apparently also of Levites, and
of other Jews.

In Ecclesiasticus the elders are no longer notables and heads of
families only; they include sages and scribes as well. Similarly the

---

[1] Cowley, AP 30, 31.

[2] Cf. J.M. Grinz, Book of Judith (Hebrew), Jerusalem 1957, 15, 105, and the bibliography indicated there, and also Bickerman, Instit. 165; Zucker, Studien 12 ff.

[3] See J. Liver, in Biblical Encyclopedia (Hebrew) II, 938-941.

History of Susanna describes how the elders of the place invite a young man to sit with them, due to his wisdom (Theodotion's version, 50).

The distinction between priests and elders was preserved also in the privilege of Antiochus III : "And the *council of elders* and the priests and the scribes of the temple and its singers shall be exempt from the poll tax" (Josephus, Antiquities XII 3.3.142).[1] In this context it is clear that the two bodies, the elders and the priests, sat within the precincts of the Temple, and this is the reason for being exempt from the royal tax.

Although by Hasmonean initiative the status of the priests was strengthened at the expense of the elders, the distinction between the elders (*presbyteroi*) and the priests is stressed from time to time in I Maccabees (VII 33, XI 23, XII 6, XIV 20, 28). As a result of the struggle between them, there afterwards arose the dispute between Sadducees and Pharisees mentioned above.

The council of elders and priests dealt with all public affairs at the side of a prince, high priest or king. It supervised the erection of the Temple (Ezra VI), it convened the people (Ezra X 8), it represented the nation *vis-a-vis* other countries and decided on matters of war (Judith IV 8, I Maccabees XII 35). As long as the priests and the elders sat separately, each body elected its own head officers, the prince and high priest; when they united Simon was elected by all of them together (I Maccabees XIV 28).

The *gerousia* issued statutes not only for the cities of Judea but even for the communities abroad, as illustrated by the letter concerning the Feast of *Hanukka*, sent on behalf of "the people in Jerusalem and Judea and the *council of elders* and Judas to Aristobulos ... and to the Jews in Egypt" (II Maccabees I 10). Similarly, from this council religious instruction went forth to all Israel, as for instance in the question of non-Levites eating of the tithes during a year of famine : "They have sent some to Jerusalem, because they also that dwell there have done this thing, to bring them a licence from *the senate*". (Judith XI 14).[2]

---

[1] Zucker, Studien, 34.

[2] For the laws of offerings and tithes at the time the book was written cf. J.M. Grinz, Book of Judith (Hebrew), 155, 189 ff. As to the authority given by the court in Jerusalem to license a prohibition if the need arises : T Shabbath XV 11-13. As to the eating of sacramental food during a year of famine see Yalkut Shimoni on I Samuel, XXI 7.

4. The Sanhedrin

At the end of the Hasmonean period the council of elders was called by the name of *sanhedrin (synedrion)*, common to Greek cities.[1] The *Great Sanhedrin* in Jerusalem comprised seventy-one men, following the seventy men who bore the yoke of the people together with Moses (Num. XI 16). Similar institutions were set up in various parts of Palestine and in Alexandria (Josephus, Wars, II 18.6.482; II 20.5.570; T Sukkah IV 6). Generally, however such sanhedrins as were set up outside Jerusalem, such as those set up by the Roman Governor (Josephus, Antiquities XIV 5.4.91), were of a smaller number of members. Such a body is known in the Mishna as a *small sanhedrin* (M Sanhedrin I 6), and such a sanhedrin may have been set up for a district or for a number of districts, for it is hard to assume that a separate one convened in each and every city.[2]

In the *Sanhedrin* the priests and the elders sat together : "The commandment to set up a court involves that there should be priests and Levites on it" (Sifre Deut. 153).[3] The elders were no longer representatives of the families but sages and Pharisees, and the priests may have been in large part Sadducees. At the beginning the priests were stronger, until the dispute broke out at the end of the days of Hyrcanus (the close of the second century B.C.E.). It was previously held that "not everyone is qualified to try capital cases but only priests, Levites and others whose families intermarry with the priestly families" (M Sanhedrin IV 2). In other words, such non-Levites who are qualified must at least be such as are eligible to marry into the priestly families. When the Pharisees gained strength during the reign of Salome (76 B.C.E.) the Sadducee priests were excluded from the Sanhedrin, and then a different interpretation was placed on the saying quoted above : "The commandment to set up a court involves that there should be priests and Levites on it : can it be said that the commandment implies that if they are not on it, it is incompetent ? Scripture says *and to the judge*—even though there are no priests and

---

[1] Of the vast literature concerning the Sanhedrin, the following may be noted here : Honig, Sanh.; Mantel, Sanh.; E. Lohse, Theologisches Wörterbuch zum neuen Testament VII 858-869; I. Baer, Israel among the Nations (Hebrew), Jerusalem 1955, 62-73; I. Baer, Zion (Hebrew) XVII (1952) 4-24; J. Efron, Doron (Hebrew) I (1967) 167-204.

[2] As to the venue of the Sanhedrin cf. J. Blinzler, Der Prozess Jesu, Regensburg 1960. 116 ff.; Lohse, *op. cit.*

[3] Compare T Sanhedrin IV 7 with TJ Sanhedrin II 6, 20c.

Levites on it—it is competent" (Sifre Deut. 153). This is a declaration
of legality of the Pharisee Sanhedrin, although the priests are not
represented on it.

In appointing the elders experience was a prerequisite : "No elder
may sit in the Stone Chamber unless he was previously a judge in
his own city, if he was a judge in his own city he may be promoted
to sit on the Temple mount, and from there to the Stronghold, and
from there to the Stone Chamber" (T Shekalim III 27). They would
sit and examine, anyone who was wise and humble and calm and
fearing sin and well matured and liked by the people, they would
appoint him in his own city, and subsequently he would be promoted ..." (T Ḥagiga II 9, Sanhedrin VII 1).[1]

Until the time of King Jannaeus the king presided over the Sanhedrin, he being also high priest. It was then held that "the high
priest may try cases and be tried" (M Sanhedrin II 1), and also that
"the king may try cases and be tried" (cf. TB Sanhedrin 19a). When
Jannaeus persecuted the Pharisees, they set up a Sanhedin of their
own, headed by a president and presiding judge (M Ḥagiga II 2). The
arrangement remained in effect even after the Pharisees returned to
the established Sanhedrin, and from the time of Herod onward the
presidency of the Sanhedrin was held by Hillel and his descendants
(TB Pesaḥim 66a; M Eduyoth V 6).[2]

In the days of Jannaeus the Pharisees declared the king and his
Sanhedrin incompetent to judge : it was held that "the king may
neither try cases nor be tried" (M Sanhedrin II 2); but no parallel
rule of halakha was enunciated with regard to the high priest.[3] It may
thus be gathered that even at the end of the Second Commonwealth
the high priest tried cases together with his fellow priests and the
Pharisee sages. It is probable that in such cases he presided, and he
may have set regularly in cases involving the Temple. To this there
is reference in the descriptions of Philo (Special Laws IV - 36, 190),
Josephus (Antiquities IV 8.14.218; XX 10.5.251) and the Gospels
(Matthew XXVI 3; Acts XXII 5, XXIII 2). When, on the other

1 With regard to the ordination of elders see H.D. Mantel, Tarbiz (Hebrew)XXXII
(1963) 120-135; H. Mantel, HTR LVII (1964) 325-46; E.E. Urbach Acts of the Israel
Academy (Hebrew) II 31-54; I. Baer, Zion (Hebrew) XXXI (1966) 130.

2 As to the election of the president of the Sanhedrin see TJ Pesaḥim VI 1, 33a, TB
Pesaḥim 66a; E.A. Finkelstein, The Pharisees and the Men of the Great Synagogue
(Hebrew), New York 1950, 6; Honig, Sanh., 74; Mantel, Sanh. 1-53.

3 But see T Sanhedrin II 15.

hand, matters of halakha were discussed, a Pharisee sage would be in the chair, with the title of president.

The functions of the Sanhedrin were extensive or restricted, as the relationships between it and the regime dictated. In the early days of the Hasmoneans the Sanhedrin served as an advisory council to the high priest, in which all public affairs were discussed. At that time the high priest would do nothing before consulting his fellow-priests and the elders. It was then, apparently, that is was held that "optional wars may be declared only by a court of 71; the city and the temple courtyards may be added to only by a court of 71, sanhedrins for the tribes may be set up only by a court of 71; an idolatrous city may be declared only by a court of 71" (M Sanhedrin I 5).[1]

From the end of the days of John Hyrcanus the king no longer sought the advice of the Sanhedrin—or he set up a Sanhedrin of his own. Even in the days of Queen Salome it is doubtful whether political powers were restored to the Sanhedrin of the Pharisees. Like any Hellenistic ruler the queen must have demanded unlimited power, and transferred to the Sanhedrin matters of worship, of the Temple and judicial powers, but not matters of government and war. Herod persecuted the sages of the Sanhedrin and replaced them with his trusted men, and even set up a special council which apparently was also called *Sanhedrin*.[2]

Synonymous with *Sanhedrin* are *the Great Court* or *the Court of 71*: this name indicates its judicial function as supreme tribunal of the land. In this matter also changes occurred in the exercise of its power, following the attitude of the government, and there is a well known question as to how long it continued to exercise its jurisdiction in capital cases.[3] Be that as it may, the Sanhedrin insisted on exclusive jurisdiction in major matters: "No tial of a tribe or of a false prophet or of a high priest may be conducted except by a court of 71 ... an idolatrous city may be declared corrupt only by a court of 71 ..." (M. Sanhedrin I 5). The *tribe here mentioned is apparently one of those* mentioned in M Ta'anith IV 5, viz., *Judah, Benjamin, Rechab, priests,*

---

[1] Cf. Bickerman, Inst. 189. This could not be said of the Sanhedrin in any later period.

[2] Schalit, Herod, 155; Zucker, Studien, 54, 62.

[3] Of the rich literature on this topic we may here note : Honig, Sanhedrin, 125 ff., 202 ff.; P. Winter, On the Trial of Jesus, Berlin 1961, 155 f; A. Schalit, Kiryat Sefer (Hebrew) XXXVII (1962) 340; D. Flusser, Tarbiz (Hebrew) XXXI (1962) 112; I. Baer, Zion (Hebrew) XXXI (1967) 117 ff.; H. Cohen, The Trial and Death of Jesus of Nazareth (Hebrew), Tel Aviv, 1968.

Levites and various families. As time went by the tribes became identified with the districts, and "Malchijah the son of Rechab, the ruler
of the district of Beth-cherem" (Neh. III 14) is apparently of the
tribe of Rechab. Again, "Rephaiah the son of Hur, the ruler of half
the district of Jerusalem" (*ibid*. III 9) is perhaps the ruler of that part
of Jerusalem held by the sons of Judah or the sons of Benjamin. If
our assumption is correct, a district or its ruler is in the category of a
tribe in this regard and may only be tried by the great court, as is the
case of the other high functionaries (prophet and high priest).

It is likely that in the early days of Hasmoneans it was also held
that "the king may only be tried by a court of 71", and this rule of
halakha was repealed after it was decided that "the king neither
tries cases nor is himself tried" (M Sanhedrin II 2).

In the same way as the question of the power to try the king, there
also arose the question of jurisdiction in matters of genealogy of
priests. The halakha vests supreme jurisdiction in the court of 71 :
"In that place there sat the *great sanhedrin of Israel* and tried cases
of priests, and a priest disqualified would dress himself in black and
wrap himself in black and go out and away" (M end of Middoth). The
stress on the words *of Israel* refers to the dispute which arose between
the Sanhedrin and the priests, and we hear of their concurrent activity
designed to protect the lineage : "The *court of the priests* would collect
for a virgin four hundred zuz, and the *Sages* did not object" (M Kethuboth I 5).[1]

Similarly, the Sanhedrin insisted on its right to approve the appointments of the king and the high priest : "And neither a king or a high
priest may be appointed except by a court of 71" (T Sanhedrin III
4). The oath administered to the high priest before the Day of Atonement accordingly ran, "we are the agents of the *court* and you are
our agent and the agent of the *court*" (M Yoma I 5). This claim, again,
was not accepted either by the Sadducee priest or by the Hasmonean
and Herodian kings.

The Sanhedrin served chiefly as an institution of religious instruction to the people : "The *Great Court in the Stone Chamber* from which
Torah goes forth to all Israel" (M Sanhedrin XI 2). The sages of the
Sanhedrin determined the halakha and demanded of the sages of the
time, members of the Sanhedrin or not, to accept their ruling. Akabia
ben Mahalalel was thus told, "Retract on the four matters (on which

---

[1] And see M Eduyoth VIII 3.

you dissented) and we will make you presiding judge for Israel" (M Eduyoth V 6).[1]

Instructions of the court were given in letters sent by its presidents to the cities of the country and also to neighbouring countries. These letters were formulated in the imperative, as befits the supreme legislating and judicial forum.[2] The wording of such a letter from the days of Simon ben Shetaḥ has been preserved: "From great Jerusalem to small Alexandria" (TJ Sanhedrin VI 9, 23c); the exaggeration here is indicative of the extent to which the Sanhedrin dominated the Jewish world. Other letters have been preserved from the days of Rabban Gamliel the Elder : "To our brethren residents of Upper Galilee and residents of Lower Galilee may your peace increase. We notify you... and to our brethren residents of the Upper South and residents of the Lower South[3]—may your peace increase. We notify you... and to our brethren residents of the exile of Babylon and residents of the exile of Media and the other exiles of Israel may your peace increase. We notify you ..." (T Sanhedrin II 6).

5. Priests and Levites

Among the returning exiles there were a few thousand priests, who traced their lineage to four priestly *houses*, and also seventy-four Levites, besides the *singers*, the *gate-keepers* and the *Nethinim* (Ezra II 36-42, Neh. VII 39-45). It is likely that the priests were gathered from among more than four *houses*, but they were organized under the patronage of four leaders only. They settled in the towns of the country and derived their livelihood from agriculture, supplemented by the gifts due to them as priests. Due to the small number of priestly *houses*, and due to the fact that some of the priests could not furnish documents of lineage, the previous division of the priests (I Chronicles XXIV) was no longer continued. Therefore Neḥemiah "appointed *wards* for the priests and for the Levites, everyone in his work" (Neh. XIII 30).[4]

---

[1] In this connection see I. Baer, Zion (Hebrew) XXVII (1962), 130; E.E. Halevi Tarbiz (Hebrew) XXVIII (1959) 154 ff.; B. de Vries, Studies in Talmudic Literature (Hebrew), Jerusalem 1968, 172 ff.

[2] As to these letters see E. Burstein, Sinai (Hebrew) XLIX (1961) 37-48.

[3] This distinction seems to follow somewhat mechanically the one between Upper and Lower Galilee.

[4] Cf. M. Haran, in Biblical Encyclopedia (Hebrew) *s.v. Kehuna;* J. Liver, *ibid., s.v.*

In several lists of priestly *families* (as in Neh. XII) there are twenty-two *families* mentioned, and it is hard to tell how they apportioned the service of the Temple during the course of the year. At about the time of Neḥemiah there was again a division, into twenty-four *wards* this time, and this arrangement remained in effect until the destruction (M Taʿanith IV 2). Accordingly each *ward* served twice a year for one week, and on the holidays all the *families* would perform their services together.

The composition of the *wards* did not remain constant either. *Families* that did not originally return from the exile were excluded from calculations, and when their members arrived later on they would be joined to one of the existing *wards*,[1] but at a later stage it was granted that the *ward* be called by their name.[2] Each *ward* would be divided into families in order that the *ward* be able to serve for one week twice a year, and each family would serve one day during that week (T Taʿanith II 1-2, TB Menaḥoth 107b). Besides these days, the priests would go up to Jerusalem on the three festivals, in order to serve according to a special drawing of lots (M Sukkah V 7). During the rest of the year the most of the priests lived in their towns all over the country and pursued their occupations, or lived on their priestly gifts (Tobias I 6-8; Judith XI 13; Ecclesiasticus VII 32-33).[3] The Persian authorities exempted from taxes all "the priests and Levites, the singers, porters, Nethinim or servants of this house of God" (Ezra VII 24), and this exemption remained in force during the Greek and Hasmonean periods. When the Sages of the Sanhedrin later on attempted to oblige the priests to pay the half shekel, the priests would invoke Scripture in their favour in order to prove they were entitled to be exempt (M Shekalim I 3-4).[4]

The *wards* of priests served as focal points for the organisation of

Mishmar; J. Liver, Chapters of the History of the Priesthood and Levites (Hebrew), Jerusalem 1969; R. de Vaux, Ancient Israel, New York 1965, 387 ff.

[1] For a parallel case, of new priestly families joining the existing ones in Egypt : W. Otto, Priester und Tempel im hellenistischen Aegypten, Leipzig-Berlin 1905-8, I, 24 ff.

[2] Cf. Lieberman, Tos. Kif., Taʿaniyoth II 1.

[3] The priestly gifts were not handed over to the priests in the periphery, but were brought to the Temple and there distributed among the priests. See Alon, Studies, I 84; E.E. Urbach, Zion (Hebrew) XVI (1951) 3-4, 11; I. Baer, Zion (Hebrew) XXVII (1962) 150; and *infra* p. 63 ff.

[4] Some of the priests of Egypt were also exempt from poll tax (*laographia*), but generally the priests in Hellenistic Egypt were subject to all taxes : Otto, Priester, II 246 ff.

the Levites and common Israelites living nearby, so much that they too were regarded as belonging to the several *wards* : "For each and every *ward* there was a representation in Jerusalem of priests, of Levites and common Israelites. When the time came for a *ward* to go up, its priests and Levites would go up to Jerusalem and the common Israelites of the *ward* would gather and read the passages concerning the Creation" (M Ta'anith IV 2). These extended *wards* may be the *acquaintances of the priests and Levites* who became entitled to one third of the tithe brought to the Temple (TJ Ma'aser Sheni, ch. V *ad fin* , 56d).[1] In this regard the *wards* resemble the Greek societies engaged in worship, with laymen participating and priests leading.[2]

Besides the *wards* in the country at large, there were families of priests and of common Israelites who inherited special functions from their ancestors : "These are the *officers* who were in the Temple" (M Shekalim V 1). A priest who inherited one of these functions would be called by the name of the ancestral head of the family. The officer would perform his function *in trust*, according to accepted practice from the First Temple (I Chronicles IX 26-31, II Chronicles XXXI 15, 18). Hence the words *officer* and *trustee* were used synonymously; thus the family of Abtinas said, when they were removed from their function of preparing the incense : "In the past our family were extremely discreet and would hand down this scroll to one another; now that they are no longer *trustees*, take the scroll and be careful about it" (TJ Shekalim V 2, 49a).

These functions bore income for those who held them.[3] In the course of time the Sages raised objections to such hereditary officers and added a condition to the rule of inheritance : "Any person with pre-

---

[1] For *makkarei kehuna*, acquaintances of the priesthood, see II Kings XII 8, Ibn Ezra on Deuteronomy XVIII 8, and also T Terumoth I 14. The sages explained the term by reference to the root *mkr* to sell, holding that the Patriarchs sold to each other : thus *makkirei kehuna* are the priests themselves; and see the commentary of R. Samuel b. Meir (*Rashbam*) to Genesis XLIX 5. It appears to me that *makkirei kehuna* are the families of other Israelites who intermarry with the priests, compare M'Arakhin II 4, Qiddushin IV 5. At a later time the representations and the wards became identified with territorial units, and then "the town of the representation" was mentioned (M Bikkurim III 2).

[2] See bibliography concerning these societies in RIDA XVI (1969) 11-19, and Otto, *op. cit.* I, 125 ff.

[3] Cf. Tarbiz (Hebrew) XXVIII (1959) 251 ; to which there should be added "Moses became rich from the chippings of the Tablets" (TJ Shekalim V 3, 49a ; TB Nedarim 38a).

cedence in succession has precedence in office, provided his behaviour
is like that of his ancestors" (T Shekalim II 15).

At the head of the priests there stood the High Priest, whose genealogy went back to the family of Zadok.[1] The function was transferred
by succession : "they all served, he and his son and his son's son"
(TJ Yoma I 1, 38c), although it was no doubt required that the son
follow the path of his forefathers. This process was interrupted by
Antiochus Epiphanes, who removed Honia from the high priesthood
and appointed his brother Jason instead (II Maccabees IV 8). In so
doing, the king acted according to the concept of the Hellenistic king-
doms, that the right to appoint high priests is vested in the king. In
Ptolemaic Egypt the king would sell the office or transfer the right of
appointment to someone else. In this way every priest became an
official of the state and maintained allegiance to the king.[2]

The Hasmonean revolt did away with the royal appointment,
holding that the high priest should be elected by the people.[3] Jonathan
the Hasmonean was accepted by the people in occupying this high
office, but he did not enter upon his duties until his appointment
was confirmed by the Syrian king (I Maccabees X 18-21). The high
priesthood was hereditary in the House of the Hasmoneans, yet Queen
Salome was able to appoint her son Hyrcanus to be high priest, although he was not next in line.[4] Her appointee was though at least of
the Hasmonean family, whereas Herod abrogated the very principle of
succession and renewed the practice of royal appointment.[5] The
annual changes of high priests, the sale of office and the appointment
of subordinate priests, which now became ordinary practice, were a
continuation of the method of the Hellenistic and Roman regimes.[6]
Generally, however, the appointees belonged to one of a small number
of priestly families who were able to furnish high priests, deputies,

---

[1] Regarding the high priests during the Second Commonwealth see Alon, Studies
I 48-76; Theol. Wörterbuch zum Neuen Testament, s.v. archihereus. As to the genealogy
traced to the sons of Zadok, see de Vaux, op. cit. 397 ff.; J. Liver, RQ VI (1967) 3-30.

[2] Otto, op. cit. I 234 ff.

[3] As to the question whether Judah the Maccabee was elected high priest, see Tcherikover, Hellenistic , 220 f.

[4] Josephus, Antiquities XIII 16.2.408. It is however possible that the lineage adducde
by Josephus was the result of exegesis of Scripture.

[5] Josephus, Antiquities XV 3.1-39; Schalit, Herod 160; Alon, Studies, I 56.

[6] Honig, Sanh. 28; Mantel, Sanh. 24; F. Pringsheim, Gesammelte Abhandlungen,
Heidelberg, 1961, II, 264 f.

administrators and treasurers.[1] The revolution of the zealots during the war of the Destruction put an end to this arrangement, and selected one priestly ward from which the high priests were chosen by lot[2].

The main function of the high priest was to supervise the Temple, he being "the ruler of the house of God" (Neh. XI 11). Ecclesiasticus (XLV 24), in describing the covenant with Pinhas, says : "Therefore for him too, He established an ordinance, a covenant of peace to maintain the sanctuary". During the course of time the High Priest designated a special official, perhaps the Deputy, to be *prostates*, to "stand at the head" of the Temple (II Maccabees III 4). Under this arrangement the High Priest would supervise all the priests, apparently assisted by priests called *Sons of the High Priest* or *Sons of the High Priests* (M Kethuboth XIII 1), who served as a Tribunal of Priests and apparently also participated originally in the Great Sanhedrin. According to the descriptions in Philo, Josephus and the Gospels, the High Priest presided over the Sanhedrin, and the Sages also admitted that he could possibly sit on the Sanhedrin (T Sanhedrin II 15).

The High Priest was most certainly at the head of the disciplinary jurisdiction of the priests [3] and he appointed the *master of the Pul* (T Kelim Baba Kama I 6), i.e. the man in charge of criminal trials, and the clerks of the court, who were mostly of the Levites.[4] The court of the priests was headed by the High Priest, especially after the Sadducees were edged out, and the Sages preserved a number of rules of halakha accepted by this court (M Kethuboth XIII 1; Eduyoth VIII 3; Rosh Hashana I 7).

The High Priest represented the people as a whole, and not only his fellow-priests. In the Book of Judith (IV 6-7) Joiachim the priest is described as chief of the army, giving orders by the advice of the Elders. In a similar description, relating to the times of Alexander the Great, the High Priest is called upon to despatch a relieving force, supply victuals for Alexander's army and look after the payment of taxes.[5] Thus the action of Mattathias and his sons is to be under-

---

[1] Compare T Menaḥoth XIII 21 : "Woe to us from the house of Ishmael b. Piabi, for they are high priests and their sons are treasurers and their sons-in-law are overseers...".

[2] Josephus, Wars IV. 3.6-8.148; J. Klausner, History of the Second Commonwealth (Hebrew), Jerusalem 1954, V 208.

[3] M Sanhedrin IX 6.

[4] Cf. Sifre Deut. XV; TB Yebamoth 86b; Josephus, Antiquities IV. 8.14.214.

[5] Josephus, Antiquities XI 8.3.317; see also Antiquities XII 4.2.136 ff. regarding the Ptolemaic period; Tcherikover, Hellenistic 132 : Zucker, Studien 31. It should however,

stood as taking over the function of High Priest. Judah carried out the function of *Anointed of War* mentioned in M Sotah VIII 1-6 and in the Scroll of the *War of the Sons of Light and the Sons of Darkness* XV.[1]

As to other functions of a high priest with initiative we may learn from the praises of Ecclesiasticus (L2-4) concerning Simon b. Joḥanan, "in whose time the House was renovated and in whose days the Temple was fortified, in whose days the wall was built, (having) turrets for protection like a king's palace; in whose time a reservoir was dug, a water cistern like the sea in its abundance. He took thought for his people (to preserve them) from robbers, and fortified his city against the enemy".

The High Priest was in overall policing charge of the markets. He was responsible for the *agoranomoi* and would appoint *agoranomoi* to supervise measures and weights, and perhaps also prices of commodities.[2] In the course of such supervision the high priests naturally saw to it that tithes and priestly gifts were duly set aside (TJ Ma'aser Sheni V *ad fin.*, 56d).[3]

6. The Temple

The returning exiles subjected themselves to a tax for the upkeep of the Temple, part *in specie* and part in wood that served to maintain the permanent fire on the altar : "Also we made ordinances for us, to charge ourselves yearly with the third part of a shekel for the service of the house, of our God ... And we cast lots, the priests, the Levites, and the people, for the wood-offering, to bring it into the house of our God, according to our father's houses, at times appointed year by year, to burn upon the altar of the Lord our God, as it is written in the Law ..." (Neh. X 33-35). In their convenant they stipulated that priestly gifts would be brought to the Temple—apparently in order to supervise

---

be noted that in Seleucid documents, just as in the decree of Darius to built the Temple, only the council of elders is mentioned as the authority of the people, see M. Stern Documents of the Hasmonean Revolt (Hebrew), Tel Aviv 1965, 32. The administrative activity of the high priest was apparently strange in the view of the Persian and Greek ruling powers, and they therefore applied to the only body which they knew.

[1] See I. Baer, Zion (Hebrew) XVII (1952) 6.

[2] As to this function see T Baba Meṣia VI 14; TJ Demai II 1.22c; Baba Bathra V 11.15a; T Kelim Baba Kama VI 19; TB Baba Bathra 89a.

[3] See Urbach, Zion (Hebrew) XVI (1951) 3-4, 11.

the fulfilment of other obligation on the part of the people, to ensure
proper distribution between the several priestly wards, and to give
special attention to the priests who lived in Jerusalem. So as to ensure
that the obligation was carried out, pairs of messengers were sent out
on circuit to attend to the setting aside of Leave-offerings for the
priests (TJ Sotah IX 11, 24a).

Originally this arrangement did not apply to tithes, which were given
over to the Levites "in all the cities" (Neh. X 38). But due to the small
number of Levites the people were obliged to bring the tithes as well
to Jerusalem, and there they were distributed to the priests and the
Levites : "Originally the tithe was made into three parts, one third
for *acquaintances of priests and Levites*, one third for the treasury and
one third for the poor and the *associates* in Jerusalem" (TJ Ma'aser
Sheni V 9, 56d). The Temple thus served as a collection center for the
Levites also (cf. Tobias I 6-8), and then the tithes were distributed
among the priests and Levites in Jerusalem and the periphery.[1]

The fruit and crops set aside as leave offerings and tithes and the
monies for the upkeep of the Temple were collected in each city, and
were then sent by messenger to the Temple (Judith XI 13; M Shekalim
II 1). Just as leave offerings were demanded by pairs of messengers
appointed for the purpose, defaulters in the payment of the Shekel
had to deposit a pledge (M Shekalim I 3).[2] Thus we find a plaint from
the end of the days of the Second Temple. "Woe to us from the house
Ishmael b. Piabi, for they are high priests and their sons are treasurers
and their sons-in-law are overseers, and their servants come and beat
us with sticks" (T Menaḥoth XIII 21).[3] A number of handles of clay
vessels have been found, inscribed with the words *for the king* or
for Jerusalem. They belong to the 3rd century B.C.E., and they probably testify to the leave—offerings and the tithes sent to the King
or to the Temple in Jerusalem.[4]

When the country grew by the added territory conquered by John
Hyrcanus, the tithes and leave-offerings could no longer be brought

---

[1] See also Albeck, Mishna, Introduction to Ma'aseroth (Hebrew). Centralisation at
the Temple is mentioned also in Malachi III 10, II Chronicles XXXI 5, Neh. X 36,
XIII 12; and cf. *Ramban* (Nachmanides) on Deut. XII 6.

[2] Cf. Philo, Laws I 78; Josephus, Antiquities XVIII 9.1.312-313. For the justification
of coercion see T Shekalim I 6.

[3] Cf. Josephus, Antiquities XX 8.8.179-181.

[4] P.W. Lapp, BASOR, 172 (1963) 22-35.

to Jerusalem, and it again became the practice to give them dirctly to the priests in the periphery. This may be connected with another practice, that of the priests who would use violence in extracting the tithes, before their owners brought them to the Temple (TJ Sotah X 11, 24a).From this time on it was no longer necessary to recite the thank-giving prayer on the presentation of tithes; it was discontinued by the High Priest, and one of the reasons may have been that they were no longer presented in the old sense (M Ma'aser Sheni *ad fin.*).[1]

The Temple also received appopriations from the Imperial treasury. Cyrus ordered that building expenses "be given out of the king's house" (Ezra VI 4, 8). Animals and food were also donated to the Temple out of the royal treasury, so that prayers should be offered "for the life of the king and of his sons"(Ezra VI 9-10). The Seleucid kings paid money to the Temple for the sacrifices,[2] and the Hasmoneans certainly did likewise.

But the main revenue of the Temple was derived from vows and freewillofferings, for the altar or for repairs. The halakha granted the Temple certain advantages so as to increase consecrated property : "The *Supreme* acquires title by money, a person—by taking possession. Oral declaration to the *Supreme* is as valid as delivery to a person" (M Qiddushin I 6) : although sale is completed in normal business transactions only when the purchaser takes actual possession, the trustees of the Temple may sue for the merchandise even if they have not taken possession but have only paid the price. The seller's mere words are in the nature of a vow for the benefit of the Temple, and he cannot retract.[3]

Moreover, in transactions with laymen the Temple authorities were always in an advantageous position : "Anyone undertaking to supply meal at the rate of four (for a sela) and the price stands at three, must supply at four; to supply at the rate of three and the price stands at four, must supply at four. If the meal becomes wormy, or

---

[1] On the other hand see TB Sotah 47b *ad fin.*

[2] I Maccabees X 39-40; II Maccabees III 3; Josephus, Antiquities XII, 3.3.140. Later on, however, perhaps as a reaction to Roman rule, sacrifices from Gentiles were refused : T Shekalim I 7, and Lieberman, Tos. Kif., *ibid.*

[3] The first rules for the execution of debts were also prescribed in connection with debts to the Temple : "A security may be exacted from anyone who owes a vow of value... announcement of sale of dedicated land is to be made sixty days, morning and evening (M 'Arakhin V 6, VI 1). The announcement was presumably followed by a procedure of sale to the highest bidder, after the fashion of Hellenistic law. In this regard see F. Pringsheim, Gesammelte Abhandlungen, Heidelberg 1961, II 267.

wine becomes sour, it is at his expense; and the money is not acquired
by him until the altar atones" (M Shekalim IV 9). The privilege of
being a purveyor to the Temple was apparently held in very high
esteem for the merchants to be willing to submit to such rules.

Hence it was also held that "dedication by mistake is valid. For
instance, if he said, "the first black ox to go out of my house is hereby
dedicated", and a white one went out—it is dedicated" (M Nazir V 1).
This rule of halakha, preserved in the tradition of the house of Shammai, goes on the assumption that everyone wants to make dedications
to the Temple, and therefore binds a person even contrary to his
stipulation.[1] The house of Hillel, however, did not consider the vow
binding in such circumstances.

In this way the Temple acquired lands, which were cultivated by
the priests, the Levites or the Nethinim for the purposes of the Temple.
Other lands were most probably leased to private individuals, either
at a fixed rate or for a fixed share of the harvest; of yet other lands
the Temple had only been given a usufruct. The trustees also grew
herds of cattle and sheep for the altar sacrifices. In this matter rules
of halakha were established to the advantage of the Temple authorities,
exempting them from priestly gifts, gifts for the poor, tithes, and
rules concerning forbidden fruit, seventh year crops, and the first-
born and tithes of animals.[2] Similarly it was held that "labourers may
not eat of dedicated dried figs, and cows may not eat of dedicated
grains" (M Me'ilah III 6). On the other hand, however, it was held
that a dedication does not supersede a prior charge : "If a person
dedicates the future handiwork of his wife, she nevertheless collects
her maintenance from it" (M Kethuboth V 4).[3]

Severe penalties were imposed during the Hasmonean [4] rebellion on
anyone who commited an offence relating to the property of the
Temple. "Anyone who steals a libation cup may be attacked by zealots"

---

[1] The example in this rule is reminiscent of the vow taken by Jephthah (Judges XI
30-31), but in this case the intent is binding even though the express terms would indicate
release. Cf. TJ Nazir V 1, 53d.

[2] Cf. Talmudic Encyclopedia (Hebrew), *s.v. Hekdesh*.

[3] Compare also : "If a person dedicated his property at a time when he is subject to his
marriage obligation (*kethubah*) to his wife"—she may collect from the property even
after dedication ; R. Eliezer ruled that "when he divorces her he must abjure all enjoy-
ment of her", so as to ensure that there is no *collusion* in defraud of the Temple (M
'Arakhin VI 1). However, see *ibid*. 2.

[4] The continuation of this mishna originated in the Hasmonean Beth Din, and it is
therefore most probable that the mishna belongs to the same period.

(M Sanhedrin IX 6).[1] Thus we learn that the general law relating to injury to property was not applied in the case of dedicated property. Thus only a person who injures *"property not subject to the law of trespass"* (Lev V 14 *et seqq.*) is liable in tort (M Baba Kama I 2) but not a person who injures property of the Temple. However, it was held by others that "if an ox of the Temple gores an ox of a layman—no charges ensue; if an ox of a layman gores an ox of the Temple, the owner, warned or unwarned, must pay the complete value of the gored ox" (TB Baba Kama 37b).

For the same reason that such an extraordinary remedy exists, dedicated property is mentioned among the things concerning which no oath may be taken," no double, fourfold or fivehold payments are exacted for their theft, a voluntary bailee takes no oath, and a paid bailee does not pay", if they are lost or stolen (M Shebu'oth VI 5).[2] It is also counted among the things "in which there is no *deceit*" (M Baba Meṣia IV 9). The treasurers and overseers must have been able to take care of the property of the Temple by other means, so much so that recourse need not be had to the general law.[3]

The Temple treasurers conducted banking business on behalf of the Temple; there was money available to them derived from the deposits of widows and orphans and some of the rich (II Maccabees III 10-11).[4] The treasurers apparently served as guardians for orphans and widows, and gave them weekly living allowances out of the deposit in the Temple. The rich who deposited money with the treasurers were most likely charged for the service, and their payments were credited to the Temple.

The rule laid down by Hillel, allowing a person *to throw money into the office* (M Arakhin IX 4) refers to a treasury conducted in one of the offices of the Temple.[5] Under this rule a deposit may be made

---

[1] In order to avoid theft the treasurers would mark Temple property with paint : "If he dedicated it they paint it with red dye" (T Ma'aser Sheni VI 4).

[2] However, see M Shekalim II 1 and TB Baba Meṣia 57b *ad fin.:* perhaps a distinction may be drawn between land and chattels on the one hand and money on the other.

[3] And perhaps a wilful embezzler is exempt from liability in tort because zealots may attack him, and thus death and payments cannot be imposed. On the other hand a person who steals a leave-offering is liable (M Terumoth VI 4).

[4] See also Josephus, War, VI 5. 2. 282; E. Schürer, Geschichte des jüdischen Volkes im Zeitalter Jesu Christi, Leipzig 1901-9, II[4], 325 ff. ; E. Bickerman, Annuaire de l'institut de philologie et d'histoire orientales et slaves VII (1939-40), 14 ff.

[5] See Lieberman, Hellenism 169. As to the practice in Greece see L. Ziehen, *s.v. Thesaurus,* RE, 2, 11, 1 ff.; and cf. also N.Q. Hamilton, JBL LXXXIII (1964), 365-372.

in favour of someone else, and "whenever he wishes he may come and take his money" (*ibid.*)

Collection of the Shekalim, the annual poll-tax, also involved the Temple in banking activities. Every year on the fifteenth of Adar"they would sit at tables in the country" (M Shekalim I 3).[1] Every table-manager would collect the Shekalim and exchange the coins. In consideration of this service he charged a *kollybon* (*agio*), which was also brought to the Temple treasury.[2] Only priests, women, slaves and minors were exempt from the surcharge (M Shekalim I 6).

It may be assumed that the Temple lent money on interest in order to increase its property : "Interest (laws apply) to the layman but not to dedicated property" (T Baba Kama IV 3). Further, the Temple treasurers would at times pay the purveyors in advance and demand a discount : "If he wished he could say to him : Pay me immediately for a lower price" (T Shekalim II 12). Such a transaction was not held to involve the interest, and laymen also made use of it, according to the precedent of the Temple.

The surplus of the office was apparently used to increase the income of the Temple : "Wines, oils and meals were bought with it, and the profit went to the Temple (M Shekalim IV 3). This refers not to partial profit derived from selling through storekeepers, but to direct sale by the Temple proper, to which all the profit accrued.[3] It was apparently possible to buy from the Temple whatever was needed for the presentation of a meal-offering, and also animals and fowls for sacrifices.[4]

In the Persian and Greek periods, when the High Priest was at the head of the people and the state included Jerusalem and Judea only, public expenditures were met by the Temple treasury : "and the aqueduct and the city's wall and towers and all its needs are maintained by the *surplus of the office*" (M Shekalim IV 2). These needs were supplied by the Temple's agents or by artisans whose wages were paid by its treasury. Among other things they would "repair the roads

---

[1] A. Gulak, Tarbiz (Hebrew) II (1931) 154-171; I. Baer, Zion (Hebrew) XXXI (1966) 133.

[2] T Shekalim I 8.

[3] On the other hand T Shekalim II 8. The Egyptian temples also sold surplus crops and other commodities : W. Otto, Priester, I, 280. The sale was effected by the officers in charge (M Shekalim V 4). In the Gospel Jesus is described as having put out of the Temple people who traded there : Mark XI 15-18.

[4] M Shekalim IV 7-8. This does not necessarily mean that the transactions were carried out in the Temple proper; perhaps sales were effected in stalls : I. Baer, Zion (Hebrew) XXXI (1966) 132-135 and bibliography there.

and the squares and the baths and attend to all public affairs and mark
the graves" (M Shekalim I 1).[1] It was probably after the state ex-
panded during the time of John Hyrcanus that such expenses had to
be borne by the residents of the city, and the Temple continued to bear
the cost of repairs only of *things instituted by the Babylonian return*
(M Nedarim V 5).[2]

The administration of Temple property comprised almost exclusively
priests, but with the rise of the Pharisees it was held that "priests,
Levites and other Israelites were qualified" (T Shekalim II 15). Besides
the heads of *wards* and the heads of families who were in charge of
the work for their appointed weeks, there were permanent officials
for the important functions, and such appointment passed by inheritance in certain priestly families (M Shekalim V 1). In addition there
was a separate financial administration, comprising at least three
treasurers and seven overseers (*ibid.* 2); these functions also passed
by inheritance. These officials received dedicated property, carried on
business on behalf of the Temple, and administered the various funds
and other property of the Temple.

Various rules of halakha were created as a safeguard against em-
bezzlement of Temple property by treasurers or trustees (M Shekalim
III 2).[3] Thus, "no public financial authority may be created with less
than two" (M Shekalim V 2), and the sale of meal, oil and wine was
separated from receipt of the price, so as to afford double checking
(M Shekalim V 4). Nevertheless the confidence reposed in the treasurers,
once they are appointed, is stressed : although money in one fund
should never be diverted to the uses of another, "no protest against
the trustees may be made in this regard" (T Shekalim I *ad fin.*), and
similarly, "no accounts may be required in charity matters of the
charity officials or in Temple property matters of the treasurers (TB
Baba Bathra 9a).[4]

---

[1] Although these rules refer to the month of Adar only, their inclusion in the tractate
of Shekalim would appear to indicate the fact that those expenditures were covered
by the offerings to the Chamber.

[2] For similar arrangements in Greece : I. Baer, Zion (Hebrew) XXVII (1962) 154.

[3] The practice has already been mentioned according to which Temple property was
painted with a special dye.

[4] See Tarbiz (Hebrew) XXVIII (1959) 251. Compare control arrangements in the
Egyptian Temples : Otto, Priester. II 123 ff.

7. The Executive Authority

After the successes of Simon the Hasmonean, the Great Synagogue decided in Elul 140 B.C.E., that "the Jews and the priests were well pleased that Simon should be their *leader* and high priest for ever, until a faithful prophet should arise, and that he should be a *captain* over them, to be overseers of works, and over the country, and over the arms, and over the strongholds, and that he should take charge of the sanctuary, and that he should be obeyed by all, and that all instruments in the country should be written in his name, and that he should be clothed in purple, and wear gold; and that it should not be lawful for anyone among the people or among the priests to set at nought any of these things, or to gainsay the things spoken by him or to gather an assembly in the country without him, or that any (other) should be clothed in purple, or wear a buckle of gold; but that whosoever should do otherwise, or set at nought any of these things, should be liable to punishment. And all the people consented to ordain for Simon that it should be done according to these words. And Simon accepted, and consented to fill the office of high-priest, and to be *captain and governor of the Jews* and of the priests, and to *preside over all matters.*

And they commanded to put this writing on tablets of brass, and to set them up within the precinct of the sanctuary in a conspicuous place; and copies of this (they caused) to be placed in the the the treasury to the end that Simon and his sons might have them" (I Maccabees XIV 41-49).[1]

The decision was adopted in the Great Synagogue of the people, in which the priests occupied an outstanding position, and which was convened because of the importance of the subject. The decision takes the shape of an agreement between the people and its leader, and follows the form of the covenant between the king and the people in the Bible.[2] Simon is not appointed king, because no true prophet is available to confirm the appointment, but also because he is not a descendant of the house of David. It was perhaps at this time that the expression "whom the Lord thy God shall choose" (Deut. XVII 15) was expounded to mean *through a prophet* (Sifre Deut. 157). Simon

---

[1] See M. Stern, Documents of the Hasmonean Revolt (Hebrew), Tel Aviv 1965, 132. Regarding this whole chapter see Zucker, Studien, 43, and Honig, Sanh., 46.

[2] See Falk, HL, 45.

was instead given the titles common in the Hellenic kingdom. He is the commissioner of the province (*hegoumenos*),[1] commander of the army (*strategos*), prince (*ethnarchos*) and head man (*prostates*).[2]

The powers mentioned in the appointment were also drafted according to Hellenistic form : Simon is responsible for the security of the State, and therefore he was apparently authorised to raise an army of paid soldiers loyal to him. Counting the years from the time of his ascension to the throne (cf. I Maccabees XIII 42), and the privilege of wearing gold and purple (cf. I Maccabees X 20), are characteristic of Greek rulers,[3] and the custom of setting up memorial tablets to appointments and deeds of the ruler, is also derived from Hellenistic sources.

The punishment decreed for disobedience of the ruler must be the result of actual cases. This was a mark of kingship granted to Simon too. On the other hand it was held : "Anyone who rebels against the *kingdom of the house of David* deserves to be put to death" (T Terumoth VII 20),[4] as if to stress that the Hasmonean rulers were not given such status. Likewise the passage in Joshua I 18, "whosoever he be that shall rebel against thy commandement ... shall be put to death" was expounded : (TB Sanhedrin 49a) : "This might be taken to include a command contrary to the Torah, therefore the passage continues, *only be strong and of good courage*".[5]

At the close of the appointment there is a hint at the dynastic principle that had previously prevailed in the high priesthood. No thought was apparently given to the possibility that Simon might leave two or more sons, and to the question whether the country should be divided between them or the function should pass to one of them. The Seleucid kings chose the second of these alternatives,[6] and their practice was followed in the Hasmonean kingdom. The problem rose after the death of King Jannaeus : "And although Alexander left two sons, Hyrcanus and Aristobulos, he bequeathed the kingship to Alexandra...

---

[1] See the article on this term in F. Preisigke, - E. Kiessling, Wörterbuch der griechischen Papyrusurkunden, Berlin 1925-31, III, 121.

[2] Preisigke, *op. cit.*, 150.

[3] Tcherikover, Hellenistic, 250.

[4] Although the precedent is taken from Joshua I 18, which of course does not refer to the house of David.

[5] The right to oppose the ruler when he offends against the law is made obvious in the Bible, especially in the advent of the prophets, and also in the Greek tradition against the rule of the tyrants.

[6] Bickerman, Inst., 18.

and Alexandra appointed Hyrcanus to be High Priest because of his age, but more because of his weakness".[1]

It must have been after the death of John Hyrcanus or of Jannaeus that the Sages held that Scripture prescribed the appointment of *a king not a queen* (Sifre Deut. 157), although they no doubt willingly accepted the separation of priesthood from kingship.[2]

Two outstanding features of kingship are not mentioned in the resolution of the people. No mention is made of a right of Simon to strike coins, since the Syrian king not allowed it (I Maccabees XV 6), and even when he did allow it Simon was not quick to take advantage of the right.[3] The injunction against contradicting him was in general terms, no mention being made of a right to enact laws (*prostagmata, diagrammata*) after the custom of Hellenistic kings.[4]

Simon and John Hyrcanus were not kings, but high priests who also performed executive functions. Only at the end of the second century B.C.E. did Aristobulos take over the kingship, as would be expected of a Hellenistic ruler : "After their father's death the eldest son Aristobulos saw fit to transform the government into a kingdom, which he judged the best form, and he was the first to put a diadem on his head, four hundred and eighty-one years and three months after the time when the people were released from the Babylonian captivity and returned to their own country.[5]

By this time the dispute had already erupted between the people, headed by the Pharisees, and the Hasmonean dynasty. In the view of the Sages, the Hasmoneans forfeited the priesthood, either due to the capture of John Hyrcanus'mother at Modi'in, or by their Hellenistic behaviour. They therefore demanded at the end of the reign of John Hyrcanus, that the Hasmoneans be content with secular government, and leave the crown of priesthood to some other family. With this dispute outstanding, John Hyrcanus drew closer to the Sadducees, and

---

[1] Josephus, Antiquities XIII 16.1.407; and compare War I 5. 1.107. A similar attempt to crown the King's widow was already made by John Hyrcanus. Josephus, Antiquities XIII 11.1.302.

[2] It is indeed an irony of history that Salome is known for her benign attitude to the Sages. As to a daughter succeeding to the crown in the Seleucid dynasty see Bickerman, Inst., 20.

[3] Tcherikover, Hellenistic, 250.

[4] But this right was not vested in the king during biblical times either : Falk, HL, 28.

[5] Josephus, Antiquities XIII 11.1.301.

rejected the Pharisees and the Oral Law which they taught by the Sanhedrin and the house of study.[1]

This dispute, no doubt, became more pronounced when Aristobulos assumed the throne. At that time it was held that *priests may not be anointed kings* (TJ Sotah VIII 3, 22c). The author of the book Testaments of the Twelve Patriarchs advocated separation of the religious and secular functions. The Hasmonean High Priest "shall be called by a new name, for a *king arises of Judah*" (Testament of Levi VIII 14). In other words, only a member of the tribe of Judah deserves to reign, and therefore the Hasmonean has been given a new title, like those mentioned above. The kingship has been given to Judah, but the king will be subject to the priest (Testament of Judah XXI 1-9). In this way the author wishes to persuade the Hasmoneans to content themselves with the priesthood, which takes precedence over the kingship, and not insist on holding both functions. The Pharisees went further, and demanded both the separation of the functions and the resignation of the Hasmonean dynasty from the high priesthood. Their view was given forceful expression in their petition to Pompey. "The people requested not to be subject to the *rule of kings* (saying) that by instructions from their ancestors they are to obey the priests of the God whom they worship, whereas (these two), although they are descendants of the priests, wish to bring the people under a different regime so that it should be servient (to them)".[2]

This resistance grew stronger during Herod's rule. Herod was considered an *Edomite slave* and unfit to reign. The Pharisees and Essenes therefore refused to swear allegiance to the king and the emperor,[3] and immediately after Herod died they again petitioned the Romans to abolish the kingship.[4]

On the other hand there were sages who did not hesitate to take part in the reading of the *King's Passage* by Agrippas and to encourage him (M Sotah VIII 8). In view of the king's good intentions they were ready to ignore his antecedents and the foreign character of his regime.

The dispute between the Pharisees and the king was connected with the attitude of the king towards the Torah. In the conception of the Greeks, the king was the *nomos empsychos*—the living law : everything the king does is lawful, and the king is the lawgiver. This doctrine

---

[1] Josephus, Antiquities XIII 10.5.288 ff.; TB Qiddushin 66a.

[2] Josephus Antiquities XIV 3.1.41.

[3] Josephus, Antiquities XVII 2.4.42; and cf. Schalit, Herod 163

[4] Josephus, Antiquities XVII 11.2.304.

was current with Ptolemaic and Seleucid kings,[1] and the kings of the
Hasmonean dynasty claimed a parallel status for themselves. Objection to this was of course raised by the Sages, who held the Torah to
be above the king and insisted that he submit himself to it.

Stress was therefore put on the ceremony symbolizing the king's
subjection to the Torah. The king must stand before the priest and
receive from him the scroll of the Torah in order to read the *king's
passage*. And "King Agrippas stood and received and read standing,
and the Sages praised him" (M Sotah VII 8).

Just as the prophets during the first commonwealth expressed
opposition to the king if he deviated from the Torah, the Pharisees
called for an uprising when the king refused to maintain Torah and
tradition. In this way they kept the commandment to disobey the
king in case he contravenes anything in the Torah.

A number of cases are known in which popular opposition took shape
on halakhic grounds. When King Jannaeus refrained from performing
the Pharisee custom of libation of water on the Feast of Tabernacles,
the people present *stoned* him with their *ethrogs*.[2] For the same reason
the Pharisees were actively opposed to Herod; Josephus reports that
they "are capable of considerable activity against a king, alert and
bold enough to fight in the open and cause damage"; and they even
refused to swear allegiance to him. [3] Especially "when these scholars
learned that the king's illness could not be cured, they aroused the
youth by telling them that they should pull down all the works built by
the king in violation of the laws of their fathers and so obtain from
the Law the reward of their pious efforts. It was indeed because of
this audacity in making these things in disregard of the Law's
provisions, they said, that all those misfortunes, with which he had
become familiar to a degree uncommon among mankind, had happened
to him, in particular his illness. How Herod had set about doing
certain things that were contrary to the Law, and for these he
had been reproached by Judas and Matthias and their followers. For
the king had erected over the great gate of the Temple, as a votive
offering and at great cost, a great golden eagle, although the Law
forbids those who propose to live in accordance with it to think of
setting up images or to make dedications of (the likenesses of) any

---

[1] H.J. Wolff, RIDA³ VII (1960) 216; Jones, Law 71; Bickerman, Inst. 11.

[2] Josephus, Antiquities XIII 13.5.372; M Succah IV 9.

[3] Josephus, Antiquities XVII 2.4.41.

living creatures. So these scholars ordered (their disciples) to pull the eagle down ... [1]

The attitude of the king towards the Torah was also expressed in his attitude towards the courts. Until the end of the reign of John Hyrcanus, the leader of the people served also as president of the Sanhedrin and the head of the judiciary. Hellenistic kings had such power,[2] and it was also accepted by Jewish tradition.[3]

Accordingly, one of the first steps taken by Jonathan the Hasmonean towards independence was that he "sat in Michmash and Jonathan started to *judge* the people and he *cleared out the wicked* of Israel" (I Maccabees IX 73).[4] These *wicked* were Hellenizers, and among the charges brought against them was marriage to foreign women. The Hasmonean court decreed : "Anyone who has sexual intercourse with a Gentile woman is liable for four offences" (TB Sanhedrin 82a).

After the clash between John Hyrcanus and the Pharisees and their expulsion from the Sanhedrin, the Sages set up a court of their own, in which of course the Hasmonean ruler took no part. It was perhaps at this time that it was held that "the king neither tries cases nor is himself tried, he testifies neither of his own will or by summons ..." (M Sanhedrin II 2), or : "The king does not sit in the Sanhedrin, and neither the king nor the high priest sit when the declaration of a leap year is discussed" (T Sanhedrin II 15).[5] In this latter norm where the king and high priest are mentioned separately, a later period is indicated, and it should rather be ascribed to the time of Salome or later on. As a result of the separation between the king and the Sanhedrin, the kings reverted to the Hellenistic custom and gave themselves the power to judge and to appoint judges. Herod, for instance, established a court of his own, besides the Sanhedrin, to which also he appointed sages loyal to him. The king's private court was based on the example of the Roman emperor, and its authority was similarly based on the *patria potestas* of the king over the members of his family.[6]

---

[1] Josephus, Antiquities XVII 6.2.150-154.

[2] Seidl, PtRG 74; Bickerman, Inst., 186.

[3] Cf. Falk, HL, 59. In T Sanhedrin II 10 King Hezekiah is ascribed the power to declare leap years, which is contrary to later halakha, see *infra*.

[4] See also Josephus, Antiquities XIII 1.6.34.

[5] But see *supra* that we assigned this rule to the time of Herod. And cf. Josephus, Antiquities XIV 9.4.168; TB Sanhedrin 19a (ascribing the event that gave rise to the rule to Jannaeus); Finkelstein, Pharisees, 856; Schalit, Herod, 33.

[6] Josephus, Antiquities XV 6.2.173; XVI 11.2.365; Schalit, Herod, 132.

Such private jurisdiction was later mentioned as an attribute of kingship, when Archelaus was accused of "dismissing a number of high officers from the army, sitting publicly on a throne, giving judgments as if he were a king...".[1] Such a private court could even determine matters of worship and of the Temple, since the king claimed the right to supervise the Temple and to appoint the High Priest. Thus the Levite singers of the Temple asked of king Agrippas "to convene the Sanhedrin and get them permission to wear linen robes on equal terms with the priests, maintaining that it was fitting that he should introduce, to mark his reign, some innovation by which he would be remembered. Nor did they fail to obtain their request; for the king, with the consent of those who attended the Sanhedrin, allowed the singers of hymns to discard their former robes and to wear linen ones such as they wished".[2]

As against such intervention, and as against any other attempt to impinge on the authority of the Sanhedrin of the Sages, the elders of the Sanhedrin would caution the High Priest before the Day of Atonement : "My Lord High Priest, we are the messengers of court and you are *our messenger* and the *messenger of court :* we adjure you, by Him who caused his Name to dwell in this house, not to change anything from what we have told you" (M Yoma I 5).

The administration in the Hasmonean state was no doubt a continuation of that of the Seleucid regime, which it replaced. Judea was divided into a number of districts (*nomoi*),[3] and the areas conquered were annexed with the status of additional districts (I Maccabees XI 34, 57). Only areas where there was no Jewish population were ruled directly by a royal *strategos* without attaining the status of a district.[4] In the days of Jannaeus the number of districts came to twenty-four, and it is likely that the number was chosen to equal the number of priestly *wards*.[5]

Thus administrative division followed the established order of the priestly families, and the boundaries of the districts were determined in accordance with the places of residence of the members of the ward

---

[1] Josephus, Antiquities XVII 9.5.232.

[2] Josephus, Antiquities XX 9.6.216; and cf. Honig, Sanh., 181; Mantel, Sanh. 70 ff.; R. Meyer, Orientalistische Literaturzeitung XLI (1938) 721.

[3] *Nomos* was the term for such units in the Ptolemaic period; in the Seleucid period the term was *toparchia :* Bickerman, Institutions 198; Schalit, Herod, 106-116.

[4] Schalit, Herod, 109.

[5] Schalit, Herod, 110.

and the representations and the *town of the representation* (M Bikkurim III 2) served as administrative center for the surrounding towns.

At the head of a number of districts a royal *strategos* was appointed, with duties which were apparently mainly military,[1] and he would operate from the most important town in the region. Under his supervision the heads of districts (*toparches*) functioned, assisted by a college of *archontes* (*koinon ton archonton*). This council may have later on been connected with the *sanhedrin of a tribe* or *small sanhedrin* (M Sanhedrin I 5-6). The implementation of the decisions of this body was entrusted to the *scribes*. Such a scribe, Ecclesiasticus says (XXXIX 4); "serveth among great men and appeareth before princes", indicating that he rises to his honourable position due to his knowledge. In the towns, also, a *council of elders* ruled, assisted by local scribes.[2]

One of the important officials was the *tax collector*, who collected duties levied on merchandise, except such as belonged to the royal household or was set aside for the Temple (M Nedarim III 4). A receipt for the payment was given on collection, specifying the name of the payer and the nature of the duty, and a metal seal was tied on to the merchandise. In the case of bridge tolls the collector would write two large letters on a paper and tie it on, and seal it on the outside; the knot would then be shown at the bridge upon arrival and the collector there would tear the knot so that it could not be used again.[3] Often enough the collector would exact a higher sum than prescribed in his instructions, and thus it was held that "it is difficult for collectors of charity and taxes to repent; they return to those whom they know, and the rest is to be used for public purposes" (T Baba Meṣia VIII 26).

Another official was the *agoranomos*, the supervisor of the market (II Maccabees III 4). His function was mainly to supervise the dealers in basic commodities and in bread, in order to prevent deceit and ensure that tithes and priestly gifts were set apart.[4]

The financial administration of the Jewish state was not developed.

---

[1] Schalit, Herod, 116-118.

[2] Schalit, Herod, 116. As to local government see *infra*.

[3] Lieberman, Tos. Kif. Shabbath VIII, p. 117; compare Matthew IX 9, Mark II 14, Luke V 27, Schalit, Herod 149 ff.

[4] I. Baer, Zion (Hebrew) XXVII (1962) 149; S. Lieberman, Tos. Kif.Nedarim, 419. King Agrippas served in his younger days as an *agoranomos* in Tiberias : Josephus, Antiquities XVIII 6. 2. 149. As to the question whether he was empowered to control prices see, for a later age, TB Baba Bathra 89a.

As long as state affairs were conducted by the High Priest, all revenue reached the Temple treasury and all expenditures were paid out of this treasury. The distribution of tithes has already been mentioned. "One third for *acquaintances of priests and Levites*, one third for the *treasury* and one third for the *poor* and the *associates* in Jerusalem" (TJ Ma'aser Sheni V 9, 56d). At that time a distinction can thus be seen to have been made between the needs of the priests and Levites, the needs of the poor and the general needs of the public. The money of the treasury was primarily used for repairs of the Temple, and "from the remainder in the office" other public needs were paid for. Josephus explains to his readers the identity of the treasury of the Temple with that of the State : "We have no public funds (*demosia chremata*) but only those of God (*tou Theou*)".[1]

To this tradition there was added, in the Hasmonean state, the precedent of the Hellenistic rulers, according to which all state revenue belonged to the king and public needs would be covered by payments from the household. The union of the functions of high priest and king enabled the system of the Temple treasury to continue, but at the same time the Hasmoneans accumulated a vast private fortune, both from the conquered territories and from duties levied on the citizens.[2] Thus although the king-high priest supervised the treasury of the Temple, it is likely that he channeled a considerable portion of the revenue to his private treasury and paid part of the administrative expenses from his household. Separation between Temple funds and royal funds may have commenced in the days of Herod.

As a result of the absence of set rules in this regard there occurred numerous cases of unjustified collections, as shown by the complaints against the brothers Hyrcanus and Aristobulos and against Herod.[3] The principle of the rule of law, and a protest against illegal collections, are both given expression in the words of the author of Joseph's Testament (XIV 5) that "among the Egyptians no such thing is done as to take the property of others before due legal proof".

8. Local Government

The returning exiles who settled in Judea round about Jerusalem were not many, and the area which they occupied was not large :

---

[1] Josephus, Antiquities XIV, 7.2.113.

[2] Schalit, Herod, 137-154; and see Bickerman, 106.

[3] Josephus, Antiquities XIV 3.1.41; XVII 11.2.304.

"So the priests, and the Levites, and some of the people, and the
singers, and the porters, and the Nethinim, dwelt in their cities, and
all Israel in their cities" (Ezra II 70). These cities were mere *townlets*,
and of course were not surrounded by walls, the building of which
involved difficulties such as were encountered in Jerusalem. The
country was divided into *districts*, perhaps even into *half-districts*
(Neh. III 9-18), and each administrative unit was headed by a governor and his officials. The status of town may have been reserved,
as time went on, to the seat of such a district governor, the other
inhabited places being called townlets.[1] Later the distinction grew
between *the town of the representation* and *the townlets within the representation* (M Bikkurim III 2). The townlets, in turn, were large in
comparision with the villages, and on *gathering days*, apparently
Mondays and Thursdays, the villagers would come to the townlets
for prayer and for marketing (M Megillah I 1), and then *courts would
sit* (M Kethuboth I 1).

It appears likely that the towns and perhaps the townlets as well,
established their own institutions, customs and statutes, and even
developed elements of democratic self-rule. For this they could, on the
one hand, follow the example of the city elders and council as they
existed before the Babylonian exile (Proverbs VIII 3, XXXI 23), and
on the other hand they may have tried to imitate the regime in the
Greek cities in Palestine.[2] This latter factor was noticeable during
and after the Greek period.

Among the requests which the Hellenistic party submitted to
Antiochus Epiphanes was "to register them as *Men of Antioch* who
are in Jerusalem (II Maccabees IV 9), that is to say, to give them the
status of a Greek city. This status was again confirmed in the days
of Jonathan the Hasmonean (I Maccabees X 31),[3] and it influenced
the internal administration of the city. The same applies to the conquest of Jaffa and Gezer by Simon the Hasmonean (I Maccabees XIII
43-48, XIV 5) : the Jews whom he settled there certainly continued

---

[1] Cf. the distinction drawn by Josephus, Life XXXVII 188 between towns and townlets in the Galilee, and the remark of Jones, Cities, 236.

[2] The example of the Greek polis certainly reached the Jews of Alexandria : Epistle
of Aristeas, 310; Josephus Antiquities XII 2.13.108. See also in general : I. Baer, Zion
(Hebrew) XV (1950) 1-18; F. Vittinghoff, ZSS LXVIII (1951), Rom. Abt. 435-85; A.H.M.
Jones, Recueil, Société Jean Bodin VI (1954) 135-176; Ch. Préaux, *ibid.* 69-133; L.
Gernet, *ibid.* VIII (1957) 45-57.

[3] Josephus, Antiquities XIII 2.3.48-57; Jones, Cities, 253.

the administrative practices of the Greek *polis*, as they found them prevailing among the previous population.

Tiberias is an example of a Jewish town administered in Greek fashion. The *men of Tiberias* or the *sons of Tiberias* (M Shabbath III 4; T Erubin V (VII) 2) were considered a municipal association, and at a certain stage even annexed the nearby Hamath : "Now the sons of Tiberias and the sons of Hamatha have again become one town" (T Erubin *ibid.*; TB Megillah 6a). The local community was called the *knesseth* (M Erubin X 10), this term being translated into Greek as *syllogos, ochlos, ekklesia*. The *knesseth* in Tiberias decided to permit certain things in the matter of *'erubin* (limitations on carrying and on walking distances on the Shabbath); perhaps dealt in general with legislative as well as judicial matters. Josephus tells of a *boule*, a council of six hundred out of a total population of more than ten thousand.[1] He also mentions ten persons, *dekaprotoi*, who were apparently chosen as leading townsmen (TB Megillah 26a/b) for one year,[2] and an *archon* at the head of the town.[3] Whoever filled this position was perhaps a scion of the family of the best lineage, and inherited the office and held it for life.[4]

The townsmen, and certainly the men of the townlets and villages, were subject to the instructions of the over-all political and religious authorities, who it may be assumed, appointed their headmen. Ezra, for instance, was granted the authority to appoint local judges "who may judge all the people that are beyond the River, all such as know the laws of thy God" (Ezra VII 25), and he charged these judges, together with the elders of the locality, to bring the offenders before him : "and let all them that are in our cities that have married foreign women come at appointed times, and with them the *elders of every town*, and the judges thereof" (Ezra X 14). It goes without saying that the governors of the towns were appointed by the governor of the land (Neh. III 19, VII 2) and received instructions from him. Even in a place where the head of the local *knesseth* was popular with the townsmen, the ruler could remove him and appoint someone else in his stead. Josephus relates how he "selected from the nation seventy

---

[1] Josephus, Wars II 21.9.641 : Josephus detains two thousand of the inhabitants most probably those fit for military service. As to democratic self-rule in Palestine see Alon, Studies, II, 15 ff.

[2] Josephus, Life XIII 69, LVII 296.

[3] Josephus, Life XXVII 134, LIV 278, LVII 294.

[4] Cf. Jones, Cities, 277.

persons of mature years and the greatest discretion and appointed them magistrates of the whole Galilee, and seven individuals in each city to adjudicate upon petty disputes, with instructions to refer more important matters and capital cases to himself and the seventy".[1] Soon afterwards the prince Rabban Gamliel assumed similar powers when "Shazfar head of Gader delayed (new moon witnesses on the way to testify) and Rabban Gamliel sent and removed him from his high office (TB Rosh Hashana 22a; TJ Rosh Hashana I 6. 57b). It has already been noted that the *knesseth* of Tiberias made a certain decision in matters of *'erubin* "until Rabban Gamliel and the elders came and restrained them" (M Erubin X 10).[2] The *wards* of priests, Levites and laymen received instructions from the officer in charge (M Tamid V 1, Biccurim III 2), and the government had frequent direct contacts with the townsmen. One important principle was joint responsiblity of the townsmen for the payment of taxes, which were collected by their own collectors and transferred to the center : "If the townsmen have sent their Shekalim and they were stolen or lost, then if the leave-offering had already been paid for out of the money—the messengers make oath to the treasurers of the Temple, and if it had not been paid for—they make oath to the townsmen, and the townsmen contribute new Shekalim instead of the others" (M Shekalim II 1).

Each town was headed, as we have seen, by an *archon* or a number of *archontes*; if indeed there were more than one it was their duty to supervise each other : "no financially dominant public office is to be given to less than two, except Ben Aḥiya... who were accepted by a majority of the public" (M Shekalim V 2).[3] In the Book of Judith (VI 14/15) three heads of towns "who existed in those days" are mentioned, and the expression may indicate that the *archontes* were elected from among the distinguished families, and perhaps for a definite period. The halakha also obliges the head of the synagogue to attention to public opinion in connection with reading the Torah in public : "The *head of the synagogue* should not read until others tell him (to do so), for one does not snatch things with one's own hands for oneself" (T Megillah III (IV) 21).

---

[1] Josephus, War II 20.5.571 : following the precedent set by Moses.

[2] Compare another order of Rabban Gamliel to the head of the knesseth of Chezib : T Terumoth II 13.

[3] Compare also M Pe'ah VIII 7. Public offices in Greek cities were also held by two people jointly.

The larger the town the more were the distinguished families who demanded that the head of the town be elected from among them. Therefore Josephus relates that Moses decreed that "as rulers at each city have seven men long exercised in virtue and in the pursuit of justice; and to each magistracy let there be assigned two subordinate officers of the tribe of Levi".[1] Josephus himself, as noted above, appointed the seven in every town in Galilee, just as the Sages of Babylon spoke later on of the *seven leading townsmen* (TB Megillah 26a/b). These were apparently selected for one year from among the leading families of the city.

A *controller* headed the Dead Sea Community as well; he was the leader of the members of the sect, and under him there were "ten men selected from the Community for the time being : four of the tribe of Levi and Aaron and from the Israelites (laymen) six learned in the Book of Meditation and the foundations of the covenant, of the age between twenty-five and sixty; and let no one over the age of sixty stand to judge the Community".[2] The composition of priests, Levites and laymen [3] indicates the guiding principle in the composition of parallel bodies in the towns, that the various families of the locality be represented in them.[4]

The *archontes* would determine all the affairs of the town, and especially would spend monies out of public funds for public needs. They were also called *parnassim* (T Megillah II 12 (III 1), either because they attended to the *pherne* (equipment) of the city or on account of their being *pronoos* (prudent).[5] The title is mainly derived from their function as collectors and distributors of charity (T Megillah II 12, 15 (III 1, 4); Shekalim I 12, II 8; Gittin V (III) 4).[6]

---

[1] Josephus, Antiquities IV 8.14.214. However the appellation "Levites" is itself apparently derived from "assistants" to the priests.

[2] Damascus Covenant X 4; compare Manual of Discipline VIII 1 : "And there were in the council of the Community twelve persons and three priests. As to the limitation of age compare TB Sanhedrin 36b : "No one who is old, a eunuch or childless may be appointed to the Sanhedrin"; TJ Sanhedrin IV 9.22b : "Even a person below twenty ... is eligible for civil cases but not in capital cases".

[3] Compare also M Sanhedrin I 3 : "(Assessment of) land by nine persons and a priest".

[4] This was the arrangement in the Greek polis : A.H.M. Jones, The Greek City from Alexander to Justinian, Oxford 1940.

[5] See the Septuagint's rendering of "he shall surely pay a dowry for her" (Ex. XXII 15), hence *pherné*.

[6] Compare also the letter of the *parnassim* of the village Beth Mishko to Joshua b. Gilgula : DJD II No. 42.

Together with the *archontes* a council of *elders* functioned in every locality, "the elders of every city" referred to in Ezra X 14, the *presbyteroi* of Judith VI 14. These elders served as judges and as accusers before higher courts (Ezra *ibid.;* History of Susanna); they constituted the "people's counsel", and could be joined by elders and sages, but not by ignorant artisans (Ecclesiasticus XXXVIII 43). A young man could also be required to sit on such a council, if he had acquired wisdom "and God had granted him age" (Book of Susanna, Theodotion's version, L).

This council may have served as an example for the *small Sanhedrin* of the Mishna (Sanhedrin I 6), representing *the community* as judge and as rescuer (*ibid.*), whose active members were about one tenth of the men in the city (*ibid.*).

The affairs of the town were at times discussed at a plenary assembly of the townsmen, the *ekklesia* mentioned in the Book of Judith.[1] Such a large forum was generally called upon to deal with capital offences, an instance of which is furnished in the History of Susanna, where the trial by the *synagogue* of the woman taken in adultery is described. Thus Ecclesiasticus says of the adultress : "She shall be led into the *assembly*, and upon her children there will be visitation" (XXIII 24).[2] A judge who preverted justice was also liable to be brought to trial before the community :"lest thou be in fear in the presence of a mighty man, and thou put a stumbling-block in (the way of) thy uprightness. Sin not against the *assembly in the gate*, that it cast thee not down among the multitude" (*ibid.* VII 6-7).[3] The townsmen also decided on administrative questions and performed executive functions, and therefore "make thyself beloved in the *assembly*, and to the ruler of the city bow thy head" (*ibid.* IV 7).

Such an assembly is depicted in the Mishna as a gathering of people listening to the discussions of the elders "A sanhedrin was like half a circular threshing floor ... and three rows of scholars would sit in front of them, each person knowing his own place; if they had to ordain they would ordain someone from the first row, and someone

---

[1] Judith VI 16.

[2] See also Ecclesiasticus XLII 11 : "Over thy daughter keep a strict watch, lest she make thee a name of evil odour—a byword in the city and accursed of the people—and shame thee in the assembly of the gate". As to trial by laymen, see G. Alon, Studies II 15 ff.

[3] Compare also Ecclesiasticus I 30 : "(Lest) the Lord reveal thy hidden (thoughts) and cast thee down in the midst of the assembly".

from the second would join the first and someone from the third would join the second, and they would choose someone from the public and let him sit in the third" (M Sanhedrin IV 3-4). "There was no further fixed seats, and whoever preceded the others to within four cubits won (his place) (T Sanhedrin VIII 2).

In the Essene community also the general membership dealt with legal cases, for "in their trials they investigate well and judge righteously, and they do not sit in judgment if their number is less than one hundred men".[1] The Dead Sea Community has a set of rules for their public assembly.[2] "This is the rule for the *public assembly*, everyone in his due position. The priests shall sit first and the elders second and the rest of the people shall each sit in his due place. And thus every judgment, counsel and matter of a public nature shall be discussed in order that everyone shall be able to give his opinion in advising the Community. No one shall enter the speech of anyone else before his brother finishes his speech, nor shall he speak before the time for his set rank. Every person shall speak in his turn when called upon. And in the *public assembly* let no one discuss any matter which is not a public concern. And the public controller and anyone who is not of the same rank as the person who happens to be raising a question for the consideration of the Community, he is to stand on his feet and say : 'I have a matter for public consideration'; if they so bid him, he may speak" (Manual of Discipline VI 8-13). Similar rules of procedure prevailed among the Sages (T Sanhedrin VII 1-VIII 2).

A synonym for the *knesseth* was the *ḥeber ʿir* (corporation of the town), which denoted especially the people locally assembled for prayer (M Berakhot IV 7). The individual belonging to such a group was called a *ḥaber ʿir* (T Megillah III (IV) 29).[3]

Although every town was subject to the central political and religious authority, no town was subject to another, and each town respected the independence of the others. In this spirit correspondence between the cities was carried on. This is illustrated at the opening of II Maccabees, where a letter is addressed, "to the Jewish brethren in the land of Egypt, the Jewish brethren in Jerusalem and the land of Judah,

---

[1] Josephus, War, II 8.9.145.

[2] As to this community see Rabin, QS *passim*; E. Koffmahn, Biblica XLII (1961) 433-442; XLIV (1963) 46-61.

[3] And cf. also Lieberman, Tos. Kif. *ibid.*, and on the passage in T Peʾah IV 16, tending to explain it as being the local committee.

good peace".[1] One generation later Jerusalem again writes to her *sister* Alexandria,[2] and thus recognizes the latter's independent standing. Later on the Sanhedrin assumed the authority to write to the Jewish towns and even to give them orders.[3] The principles of independence and non-intervention of cities are expressed in the rule of halakha : "An outcast for his own town is not an outcast for another town; an outcast for another town is not [4] an outcast for his own" (TB Mo'ed Katan 16a), indicating that a town can bind its own people but not those of another town.

The obligation of a person to participate in public affairs are determined by his domicile and not by his origin : "How long should he be in the town in order to be considered one of the townsmen ? Twelve months. If he buys a dwelling house he shall be considered one of the townsmen immediately" (M Baba Bathra I 5).[5] It may be assumed that his rights to participate in the general assembly were also determined accordingly, although in this regard there may have been families that were considered eligible and others that were not. Women, slaves and minors certainly never took part in the public discussions; and although there were towns where Jews and Gentiles lived together, the latter were not taken into account when the Jews were in the ascendant.

In each town not everyone was equal. Only some were considered "worthy of being appointed to public office" (TB Gittin 60a), because of their wisdom and ethical qualities or because of their family status. Decisions of the townsmen were adopted by a majority, and the minority could be forced to accept the majority's decision.[6] In this way the rules of halakha are construed with regard to the extent of the authority of the townsmen (T Baba Meṣia XI 23). The rule is required when there is objection to the decision of the majority, and it provides that the townsmen, meaning the majority, are *authorized* to do the thing despite the opposition of the individual. It is in this

---

[1] Cf. I. Baer, Zion (Hebrew) XV (1950) 15.

[2] TB Sotah 47 (according to the Amsterdam edition); TJ Ḥagigah II 2, 77d; Z. Frankel Ways of the Mishna (Hebrew), 35; I. Baer, *ibid.*

[3] Baer, *ibid.*

[4] Thus in the Munich MS and in Annotations of Mordecai, see Baer, *ibid.* 7. According to the current versions, ostracism of a person pronounced in his own city is valid everywhere, the local court being competent *ad personam* and no city is competent to impose such a sanction beyond its own limits on a non-resident.

[5] On the other hand see T Pe'ah IV 9.

[6] See A.H. Freimann, Yavne (Hebrew) 1948; I. Baer, Zion (Hebrew) XV (1950) 7-8.

context that R. Ishmael b.R. Yosse tells the dissenting judge : "Do
not say *accept my view*, for they have the authority, and not you"(M
Aboth IV 8).[1]

An individual who refuses to carry out the decision of the public
is to be coerced (M Baba Bathra I 5, T Baba Meṣia XI 23). Such coercion
took many forms, as the need of the hour required; the townsmen
could take from such a recalcitrant person security for performance,
or could even have him whipped. But the typical penalty for a townsman who acted contrary to a decision was ostracism, under which all
members of the community would keep away from the offender as
though he were unclean. Such a decision was binding for all the townsmen, and anyone not observing it was himself punished : "The townsmen may say : anyone appearing at X's will pay so and so much"
(T Baba Meṣia *ibid.*), apparently after X was ostracised by the townsmen. This was the penalty imposed upon anyone who breached "the
counsel of the princes and the elders" in the days of Ezra, *viz*, that
"all his substance should be forfeited, and himself separated from
the congregation of the captivity" (Ezra X 8). This sanction was
known in the Pharisee order, where the offender was declared unclean
and ostracized,[2] and was also accepted in the Dead Sea Community.[3]

Public prayer was one of the important purposes of the organisation of the townsmen, and a considerable part of their expenditure was
devoted to this purpose. "And what is *property of the town ?* Such as
the square and the bath-house and the synagogue and the ark and
the scrolls" (M Nedarim V 5).[4] Therefore *"the townsmen coerce each
other* to build them a synagogue and to buy them a scroll of the Torah
and Prophets" (T Baba Meṣia XI 23). The townsmen would also transit
their Shekalim to the Temple collectively (M Shekalim II 1), and
naturally attend to other ritual matters which required joint action.

The collection and distribution of charity was of special importance.
Assessments of charity were made in the synagogue (T Shabbath XVI
(XVII) 22, Terumoth I 10); the collectors decided how much each
townsman would have to give. Collections would be either of money
for the community fund or of food for the public kitchen; and money
from the fund was distributed to the poor of the town every Friday

---

[1] On democracy in trade unions see RIDA XVI (1969) 11 ff.

[2] Cf. Finkelstein, Pharisees, 77.

[3] Manual of Discipline VI 24-VII 25 : compare Josephus, War II 8.8.143.

[4] Compare M Megillah III 1; T Megillah II 12 ff. (III 1 ff.).

and food from the kitchen was given to any poor person every day
(T Pe'ah IV 9-10). Special appeals were also made before the holidays
(T Megillah I 5), to marry off orphans (T Shabbath XVI (XVII) 22)
or to redeem captives (T Terumoth I 10).

In Jerusalem it was apparently the rule before the Hasmonean
period "to appoint teachers of children", and after further areas were
added to the state "it was enacted to appoint (teachers) in each and
every district and (the children) were brought (to them) when they
were sixteen or seventeen years old ... until R. Joshua b. Gamla
came and introduced a change, that teachers of children be appointed
in each and every region and town and that (a child) be brought
(to them) at the age of six or seven" (TB Baba Bathra 21a).[1]

Another function with which some of the towns were charged was
"to build high walls, gates and bars" (M Baba Bathra I 5), and apparently also to provide night watchmen as the need arose (Neh. IV).
They would also "repair the roads and streets and ritual baths and
attend to all public affairs" (M Shekalim I 1).[2] For the supervision of
storekeepers they would appoint an *agoranomos*, and various statutes
were made for the maintenance of good order : "The townsmen may
determine commodity prices, and measuremants, and rates of wages.[3]
They may rescind or suspend their own statute. The townsmen may
say, whoever appears at X's or on the premises of the ruling power
shall pay so-and-so much, and the owner of a cow who grazes among
the seeds shall pay so-and-so much" (T Baba Meṣia XI 23).

Prices and wages so determined were maximum rates, calculated
to protect the townsmen against exorbitant demands The power of
the townsmen to rescind or suspend also apparently refers to economic
matters. The prohibition against appearing at X's has been explained

---

[1] Cf. F.H. Swift, Education in Ancient Israel from Earliest Times to 70 A.D., Chicago,
1919; L. Dürr, Das Erziehungswesen im A.T. und im antiken Orient, Leipzig (MVAG 36)
1932.

[2] This mishna dates back to pre-Hasmonean times, when officers of the Sanhedrin
could accomplish all these affairs. After the state was enlarged it is most likely that
such affairs were no longer attended to by messengers of the court in Jerusalem, but
rather by the leading townsmen of each town. Compare also M Mo'ed Katan I 2.

[3] In TB the expression used is *lehasia' 'al qiṣathan*, and I find it reasonable to explain
this following the Damascus Covenant I 16 : "*lassi'a gebul*" : to contravene the law—
meaning the authority of the townsmen to act in contravention of a law they had previously made or to provide for punishment of offenders. See also I. Baer, Zion (Hebrew)
XV (1950) 2.39.

above, the prohibition of appearing on the premises of the ruling power is designed to prevent intimacy with it (M Aboth I 10).[1] The penalty provided in the case of the owner of the cow who grazed in another's field is designed to simplify proceedings and to release the owner of the seeds from the onus of proving his exact loss. Similarly it was decreed in Jerusalem that "a plant of one year (would be assessed at) two pieces of silver; of two years -(at) four pieces of silver" (TB Baba Kama 58b). Such a law was required so that the owner of the seeds would not resort to self-help (cf. TB Baba Meṣia 31a) but would return the cow to its owner (T Baba Meṣia II 19).

Rules of halakha like those in the two first chapters of Baba Bathra and at the end of 'Arakhin were laid down in certain towns in the country, and the Sages later included them in their tradition. An example of local halakha is preserved also in T Baba Meṣia XI 27 : "A public bath attendant or public barber or public baker, in a place when there is no other, who wishes to go to his own house in view of an impending holiday, may be prevented from doing so until someone else takes his place; but if he has stipulated in this regard before a court, or has been mistreated by them, he may prevail".[2]

9. The Town Court

In the days of the Return to Zion the priests still served as teachers and judges for the people, and this function remained in their hands during the Greek period, and perhaps even in the early Hasmonean period. Ecclesiasticus still describes Aaron the Priest as the father of judges : "He gave him His commandments, and invested him with authority over statute and judgment, that he might teach His people statutes, and judgements unto the children of Israel" (XLV 17). Although he speaks of instruction and not of adjudication proper, it is only natural that the experts in law were themselves judges. Thus the author of "Levi's Testament" (VIII 17) also says that "of them there will be priests and judges and scribes and according to their word the sanctuary shall be guarded".

Later on, when scribes of non-priestly descent also engaged in the

---

[1] For the identity of *malkhuth* and *rashut* see M Sanhedrin VII 3 and T Sanhedrin IX 10. As to the prohibition itself against recourse to foreign courts see Mekhilta on Mishpatim (first lines) and I Corinthians VI 1-5.

[2] See RIDA XVI (1969) 11 ff.

Torah and in law, the tradition was maintained to include priests in the courts. The committee of the Dead Sea Community was composed, as mentioned above, of "four of the tribe of Levi and Aaron and six from (other) Israelites" (Damascus Covenant X (4)), and similar compositions were accepted by the Sages as well if the case affected the Temple (M Sanhedrin I 3). The judicial function of the priests was especially preserved in capital cases, and it was therefore held that "not everyone is qualified to try capital cases but only priests, Levites and other Israelites who intermarry with the priesthood" (M Sanhedrin IV 2).

The priests who sat in judgment were assisted by Levites : "Originally officers were appointed from among the Levites only" [1] (TB Yebamoth 86b). To this function again, only members of distinguished non-Levite families could originally aspire : "A person whose ancestors are known to have been public officers and collectors of charity may intermarry with the priesthood" (M Qiddushin IV 5). But until the destruction of the Second Temple the Levites were given preference, as Josephus relates : "Every person in authority is given two assistants of the tribe of Levi".[2]

But the power of the priests and the Levites was restricted from two directions : the central leadership and the local community. The Persian ruling power instructed Ezra to appoint judges (Ezra VII 25), and he appointed judges for each town from among its own elders (Ezra X 14). It is probable that the right to appoint local judges was mentioned in privileges given to the Jews by the Greek ruling power, and in those days the high priest exercised the right. With the rise of the Pharisees there undoubtedly was a dispute as to the right to appoint judges, until the Sanhedrin prevailed and it appointed the people it considered qualified : "And from there they would send and inquire—anyone who was wise and calm and fearing sin and well matured and liked by the people, they would appoint him a judge in his own city" (T Sanhedrin VII 1) or "the court appointed him over the public" (T Ta'aniyoth I 7).[3] In the days of Rabbi Akiba the judge so appointed was called *mumḥe le- beth din* (a judge qualified by court) (M Bekhoroth IV 4).[4]

---

[1] The passage goes on to rely on a presumed quotation from Scripture "the officers the many heads over you", implying that now officers are appointed by the will of the many and not according to their lineage.

[2] Antiquities IV, 8.14.214.

[3] See *supra* p. 54 ff., and see J. Ostrow, JQR XLVIII (1958) 360 ff.

[4] The *mumḥe le-beth din* is a person whom the court has assigned to the townsmen as a qualified judge. As to the title *mufla shel beth din* see Mantel, Sanh. 135 ; S.B. Honig,

At the same time the authorities in each town dealt with civil and even criminal cases. Among the statutes ascribed to Ezra was one whereby on Mondays and Thursdays a portion of the Torah was read in public and cases were tried (TB Baba Kama 82b).[1] These two days were the *days of gathering*" (M Megillah I 1) on which the villagers came to the towns "and in which *courts would sit in the towns*" (M Kethuboth I 1, T Ta'aniyoth II 4). A distinction should apparently be drawn between the judges in the cities, who were appointed, as indicated, by the central leadership,[2] and the courts that sat in the towns on the days of gathering only. These courts were composed not of professionals but of laymen, and were chosen from among the local elders. For this reason such judges were not allowed to sit alone, and each case was tried by a panel of three (M Sanhedrin I 1-3).

The judges were apparently elected from time to time by the assembly of the townsmen, and Ecclesiasticus VII 6-7 warns that one should not submit one's own candidature unless one is qualified : "Seek not to be judge, lest thou be able to eliminate evil, (and) lest thou be in fear in the presence of a mighty man, and thou put a stumbling block in the way of thy uprightness. Sin not against the *assembly in the gate*, that it cast thee not down among the multitude". The judge should also verify with whom he is to sit : "Do not sit in judgment with a judge who does wrong, for you will decide with him according to his will" (*ibid.* IV 29).[3]

A similar description is found in the Story of Susanna 5-6 : "In that year two of the elders of the people were appointed judges ... of the oldest of the judges who appeared to be leaders of the people. Even from other towns disputes were brought before them." Here it is unclear whether only two men chosen, or whether the narrative refers to two of the chosen judges. The latter version is preferable, for it is unlikely that an evennumbered court would be chosen. These judges

---

Sanh., 76; H. Mantel, HTR LVII (1964) 329 ff.; Albeck, Mishna, Horayoth I 4—Addenda (Hebrew). If we accept the explanation offered by J. Rabinowitz in Leshonenu (Hebrew). XVIII (1952) 25, that the *mumḥe le-beth din* is the equivalent of *nomophylax*, the term implies the supervision imposed on the courts in Greek times. The appointment was made by the High Priest, perhaps with the consent of the elders, according to Greek practice. See Wolff, Justizwesen, 36.

[1] And cf. TJ Megillah IV 1. 75a.

[2] Sifrè Shofetim 144.

[3] Compare TB Sanhedrin 23a : "The pure-minded people of Jerusalem ... would not sit in judgment unless they knew who was sitting with them".

apparently tried civil cases of the townsmen, and at times even civil cases of the people from out of town. On the other hand, capital cases, like the case of Susanna had to be brought before the whole community : "And they came to the meeting place of the city where they dwelt and all the children of Israel who were there gathered together" (17). In this case the elders acted as accusers and as witnesses, and the community as judge : "And all the community believed them, for they were the elders and judges of the people" (30).

Capital cases later on were tried, instead of by the community by the *small Sanhedrin*, representing the local community (M Sanhedrin I 4, 6). The more the Pharisees gained influence the less authority was left to the lay judges : the power to try cases was vested in the *Great Sanhedrin* [1] or in the qualified judges.[2] Many matters remained within the jurisdiction of the lay judges (M Yebamoth XII 1), and they continued to compete with the jurisdiction of the Sages. The status was created of a *mumḥe la-rabbim* (publicly acknowledged judge) (T Sanhedrin V 1), a trained judge who derived his authority from the public, as distinct from the *mumḥe le-beth din* mentioned above.

For such judges, who received neither their authority nor their appointment from Jerusalem, the Sages laid down a number of rules regarding their qualification and disqualification : "This is the rule : anyone suspected of being prone to an offence neither try a case involving that offence or testify in such a case" (M Bekhoroth IV 10); such a rule was required in respect of laymen but not in respect of the Sages. The *makers of decrees* in Jerusalem [3] would be paid ninety nine manehs from the offerings of the Chamber" (TB Kethuboth 105a); but the Sages forbade the lay judges to accept any pay : "Anyone who accepts pay for trying cases—his judgments are void, for testifying— his testimony void" (M Bekhoroth IV 6). At first this injunction was not a matter of law, but it was only held that is was "highly improper for a judge to accept pay or for a witness to accept pay for his testimony" (T Bekhoroth III 8).[4] But after it was decided to apply the

---

[1] As to concentration of authority to try capital cases in the court in Jerusalem see Alon, Studies, I 92 ff.

[2] As to comparison between the qualified judges and the lay judges see Alon, Studies II, 15 ff.

[3] As to the proper reading of this passage see J.N. Epstein, Tarbiz (Hebrew) I (1930) 131, and cf. E.E. Urbach, Tarbiz (Hebrew) XXVII (1958) 173; M. Baer, Bar Ilan (Hebrew) II (1964) 138; and also A Gulak, Elements of Jewish Law (Hebrew), Berlin 1923, IV 21.

[4] Amended version, according to S. Lieberman, Tosefoth Rishonim, *ibid*. In ancient Roman law also the judge was not paid : Kaser, RZPR, 9.

rule more strictly, this prohibition was included among the things that disqualify a judge even on suspicion : "Anyone suspected of accepting pay and trying cases (or accepting) pay and testifying all the cases he tried and all the testimony he gave are void" (T Bekhoroth III 8).

Further : the Sages not only denied such judges the right to be paid, but they also made them liable for mistakes in law : "If he tried a case and found the wrong party in the right or the right party in the wrong, or the pure impure or the impure pure—what he did is done, and he shall pay from his own house" (M Bekhoroth IV 4). Rabbi Akiba absolved the *mumḥe le-beth din* from liability (*ibid.*), but the laymen remained liable. By such provisions the Sages carried out their intention of severly restricting the number of laymen prepared to serve as judges.

However there were not always Sages to be found in each and every town, and thus the jurisdiction of the lay judges continued. Mention has already been made of the local judges before whom cases were brought from out of town : they thus acted as arbitrators by consent of the parties. With regard to arbitration it was said about the time of the Destruction : *"Justice justice shalt thou follow*— seek out a fitting court, the court of Rabban Johanan b. Zakkai or the court of Rabbi Eliezer (Sifre, beginning of Shofetim). In that period civil cases were generally tried by arbitrators, so much so that a fixed formula for a submission came into being (M Moʻed Katan III 3, Baba Meṣia I 8, Baba Bathra X 4).[1]

---

[1] In regard to arbitration see Alon, Studies II 44 ; Cohen, JRL, 651 ff., who ascribe it to early times. On the other hand, A. Gulak, Elements of Jewish Law (Hebrew), IV 30, and Z. Warhaftig, Rabbi Herzog Volume (Hebrew), Jerusalem 1965, 517-527, assign the advent of arbitration to the reign of Hadrian. As to forms of submissions see TB Baba Meṣia 20a. And compare the description of Hellenistic bills of submission in the article by J. Modrzejewski in JJP VI (1952) 239-256. As to arbitration in Greek law : A. Steinwenter, Die Streitbeendigung durch Urteil, Schiedsspruch und Vergleich nach griechischem Recht, MB 8, München 1925.

CHAPTER FOUR

PROCEDURE

1. Self-help

Two contrary ideas vied with each other in the Second Commonwealth, just as in the days of the Bible [1] and in other jurisdictions: [2]
on the one hand a man must be vigilant in defending his rights and
the maintenance of law in the world, and if he holds his peace or waives
a right—he is responsible for what he does and can have no complaint
against anyone else. On the other hand no one person can be plaintiff
and judge at the same time, and therefore the individual is required
not to take the law into his own hands, but to go to law. Between these
two extremes there are various compromises possible : an individual
may be allowed to come to his own rescue in certain matters specified
by the law, he may be allowed to do so within certain limits, and
perhaps he may be allowed to act only if specially authorised by court.
The Jews who returned from captivity were acquainted in Babylon
with an ordered system of adjudication, and they would not tolerate a
situation where "everyman did that which was right in his own eyes."

Indeed, punishment by individual action was common even in the
field of criminal law. When the Septuagint, in translating the passage
concerning enticement to idolatry, came to the words "but thou shalt
surely *kill him*" (Deut. XIII 10) they changed the meaning and translated *anangelon anangeleis peri autou*, as if instead *kill* the word was
report, The same interpretation is preserved in Sifre on the passage;
"if you know anything against him you may not *keep silent*", and the
reason is that in normal conditions *he is brought to court* (M Sanhedrin
VII 10) and no private punishment is allowed. [3]

But is was not always that such punishment for enticement at the
hand of a court could be anticipated. During the Hasmonean revolt

---

[1] Cf. Falk, HL 67; Cohen, JRL. 624 ff.; G.R. Driver & J.C. Miles, The Babylonian
Laws, Oxford 1952-55, I, 497 f.

[2] For recent literature on the subject see : E. Gerner, ZSS LXVII (1950) 1 ff.; Wolff,
Beiträge 1-90; J. Modrzejewski, TRG XXXI (1963), 107 ff.; Kaser, RZPR, 19 f.; 104 n. 4.

[3] There may also exist a tradition which does not require that such a case be brought
to trial in court : Alon, Studies, I 103.

it was therefore held : 'Anyone who steals a holy jar, or curses by magic,[1] or has intercourse with an Aramean woman,[2] *zealots may kill him...* If a priest functioned when impure, his fellow-priests would take him out of the courtyard and kill him off with branches" (M Sanhedrin IX 6). Similar action ignited the rebellion against the Hellenizers : "a Jew came forward in the sight of all to sacrifice upon the altar in Modi'in in accordance with the king's command. And when Mattathias saw it, his zeal was kindled, and his heart quivered (with wrath); and his indignation burst forth for judgment, so that he ran and slew him on the altar; and at the same time he (also) killed the king's officer who had come to enforce the sacrificing, pulled down the altar, and (thus) showed forth his zeal for the Law, just as Pinehas had done in the case of Zimri the son of Salome". (I Maccabees II, 23-25).

Philo of Alexandria justified such actions, calculated to eradicate alien worship from Israel, and he invoked the authority of precedent in the case of Pinehas.[3] It is probable that following the Hasmonean revolt the tradition became firm which permitted every individual to act like the zealots against idolaters.

Similar rules of halakha were created in periods of wars and of violence : "And these may be *saved from crime* even at risk to their lives : a person pursing another in order to kill him, pursuing a male (for sodomy) or pursuing a betrothed damsel" (M Sanhedrin VIII 7). [4] Acts of zeal and of *saving* people from crime probably became intensified during the war of destruction, to the extent that the power of the courts decreased and that of the zealots became greater. Then it was held "What authority (is there in Scripture) that if you cannot inflict the mode of death penalty provided for him, you should put

---

[1] A derogatory way of saying "blesses by an alien god".

[2] Of the Seleucid kingdom.

[3] Laws, I 54 ff.; cf. Alon, Studies, I 98-106; I. Baer, Zion (Hebrew) XXXI (1966) 144, 152; Cohen, JRL *loc. cit.*; M. Hengel, Die Zeloten, Leiden 1961, 151-234.

[4] This is an ancient rule of halakha, to which there were subsequently added other classes of persons who are to be saved at risk to their own lives; thus "R. Elazar b. Zadok says : the idolater" (T Sanhedrin XI 11).The sage in the Mishna referred to in the text held differently : "but a person pursuing an animal, or desecrating the Sabbath, or worshipping idolatrously—is not to be *saved at risk to his own life*". These rules are, included in M Sanhedrin VIII 7 among measures of prevention and not of punishment and are therefore placed after the rules concerning stubborn and rebellious sons and concerning housebreakers, both of whom are dealt with to avoid subsequent criminality.

him to death by any mode provided for in the Torah, whether severe or light ? Scripture says : thou shalt surely smite" (Sifre on Re'eh 94).

The Damascus Covenant, in opposing licence in matters of law or in opposing legal action being brought to Gentile tribunals, provides that "anyone attaining anything from anyone else *by the laws of the Gentiles* is worthy of death" (IX 1),[1] and we have already mentioned above the statute of the townsmen that "whoever appears ... on the premises of the ruling power shall pay so-and-so much" (T Baba Meṣia XI 23).

Particularly in civil cases a certain amount of self-help is allowed. Hillel ruled with regard to houses in walled cities that a seller who wishes to redeem what he has sold "may throw his money into the office and break the door (of his house) and enter. Whenever the other so wishes—he may come and take his money" (M Arakhin IX 4). The seller does not ask that the messenger of the court enter first; he does not even require any special authorisation from the court; he does himself what is necessary. Similarly "Ben Bag Bag says, let no one steal his own from the house of the thief, lest he himself look like a thief : let him rather break (the thief's) teeth and extract his own from (the thief's) hand" (T Baba Kama X 38).[2]

Not only for the recovery of a specific item of property but even to collect a mere debt, a man might take the law into his own hands. A strict interpretation was therefore placed on the provision of Scripture : "thou shalt not go into his house to fetch his pledge : it is his house which you may not enter, but you may enter the house of a guarantor ... (or to fetch a pledge to ensure) payment for a porter, for a donkey-driver, for lodging at an inn, for painting of portraits" (TB Baba Meṣia 115a). What is meant here is collection not through court, which is justified except for the case specified in the passage Deut. XXIV 10f. The creditor, moreover, may arrest the debtor to

---

[1] Cf. P. Winter, RQ 21 (VI, 1967) 131-36; J. Rabinowitz, RQ 23 (VI, 1968) 433-35.

[2] And cf. TB Baba Kama 27b. A reference to self-help may be seen in the expression used by Judah b. Tabbai : "the verdict having been acquiesced in by them" (M Aboth I 8). Such acquiescence resembles the *deed of renunciation* written by the party who has lost in court (Cowley, AP 6; Yaron, Introduction, 34). Thus the judge does not oblige the one party to go and give the property to the other party, but he does oblige him to submit to the decision and to raise no objection to execution of judgment by the other party. For a similar practice under Ptolemaic law see Wolff, Beiträge, 110 f. A similar system serves as a basis for the proverbial poor man's lamb (II Samuel XII) and for the judgment of the keeper (I Kings XX 40) : the judge tries to bring the accused to submit to the judgment.

extract payment of the debt : "He who *strangles a person* in the street,
and another person saw him and said he should leave him ... "(M Baba
Bathra X 8). The practice of imprisonment for debts was known,
though not recognized by Halakha.[1]

Sometimes the debtor took upon himself from the beginning that
the creditor might collect what is due to him without an order of
court. Thus self help became justified by convention. In Aramaic
promissory notes from Elephantine the lender is authorised by the
borrower in the following terms : "You, Meshullam, and your children
have the right *to take for yourself* any security which you may find of
mine in the counting-house, silver or gold, bronze or iron, male or
female slave, barley, spelt or any food that you may find of mine, till
you have full payment of your money and interest thereon".[2] This was
the prescribed form for use in regard to both small and large debts,
with the avowed aim of allowing the creditor to take the law into
his own hands.

Before the time of Simon b. Shetaḥ it was common practice to make
the property of a borrower liable for his debt, and the lender was
entitled to direct access to the property so charged, with no court
procedure involved (M Baba Bathra X 8 ; T Kethuboth XII 1). At about
that time Syllaeus borrowed money from Herod, and it was "stipulated
that when the time-limit expired, Herod should have the right to
recover the amount of the loan from all of Syllaeus' country, where-
fore ... the expedition (of Herod) was not really an expedition but
merely a *justified attempt to recover* his own money. And even then he
had not done this hastily nor as promptly as the contract allowed ..."
Since Syllaeus had not carried out his duty under the contract "Herod
again went to the governors, and when they gave him permission
to recover the money owed him, even then it was with reluctance that

---

[1] Regarding imprisonment of debtors in the Bible see : Falk, HL 100, and for the
Talmud : Gulak, Obligation 18; J. Guttmann, Dinaburg Volume (Hebrew), Jerusalem,
1960, 81 ; E.E. Urbach, Zion (Hebrew) XXV (1960) 147; Cohen, JRL, 168 f. ; M. Elon
Individual Freedom in the Methods of Debt Collection in Jewish Law (Hebrew), Jerusalem
1965, 503; R. Taubenschlag, The Law of Greco-Roman Egypt, New York 1944, 529;
Theodorides, RIDA³ V (1958) 65 ff.; Seidl, Pt RG, 103 ; J. Modrzejewski, Recherches de
papyrologie II (1962) 75-98. For imprisonment of debtors in the Gospels see : R. Sugranyes,
Etudes sur le droit palestinien à l'époque evangélique, Fribourg 1946; W. Nörr, ZSS
LXXVIII (1961) 135 ff.

[2] Cowley, AP No. 10, and cf. Yaron. Introduction, 96, construing the clause in a
stricter sense. For the collection clause in Hellenistic law see : H. Kupizewski, Eos
XLVIII, 3 (1957) (=Symbolae R. Taubenschlag) 89-103; Wolff, Beiträge, 102.

he took the field with a few men". Thus Nicolas presents Herod's case to Caesar : "And so 'the war', as these men theatrically called it, and the expedition were of this nature. And yet, how could it be a war when your governors permitted it, when the *agreement provided for it* ...".[1] In this case Herod first applied to the governors, and only afterwards went to recover his debt, but such conduct was extraordinarily cautious, and does not reflect the strict sense of the law. Enforcement against the body of the debtor, by detention in the house of the creditor, may also have been justified by an appropriate clause in the bill of debt. One of the forms by which a man could become a Hebrew slave was by selling himself to satisfy his debt, and it may be assumed that such sale was effected when the loan was made, against the eventuality that the borrower may not be able to pay the debt when due. Such a stipulation was calculated to save the creditor the trouble of prior application to court. Instead of the debtor himself a member of his family could also be given as a *hypoteke* against eventual non-payment. To a case in point, which perhaps was taken from the legal practice of Greek cities, "there testified R. Yosse the priest and R. Zachariah, son of the butcher, ... a girl *was mortgaged* in Ashkelon, and her family rejected her" (M Eduyoth VIII 2).

It may be assumed that with the passage of time the law was settled that self help would not apply to land, especially if the claim was in tort and not in debt. With regard to tort it was held that a *monetary assessment* was required (M Baba Kama I 3), and that "the court does not award assessed damages except against property that may be held liable. If the injured party seizes chattels, assessment may be made against them." (T Baba Kama I 2). The court would help the injured party to recover out of real property only; if he wanted to recover out of chattels he would have to seize them himself and then apply to court for subsequent approval.

That this principle applied also to recovery of debts is proved by the *prosbolé* procedures.[2] "This is the substance of the *porosbolé* : I deliver to you, X and Y judges in locality Z, in order that any debt due to me may be recovered by me at any time I wish. And the judges sign at the foot, or the witnesses" (M Shebi'ith X 4). Here a known formula was used so that debts might be recovered after the year of release; but the form itself is one of a *notice* given to court that the

---

[1] Josephus, Antiquities XVI 10.8.343 ff.; Gulak, Obligations, 126 ff.

[2] Regarding the *prosbolé* see *infra* p. 109.

creditor is about to recover his debt, and not a *request* for authority to do so. The *prosbolé* is thus not the equivalent of an *enechyrasia*, which authorises the creditor to recover his debt (T Baba Bathra XI 5).[1] The *prosbolé* is subject to the rule that the court requires advance notice of recovery out of real property, whereas against chattels the creditor must take direct action; therefore "a *prosbolé* may be written only against land" (M Shebi'ith X 6). Thus also the Sages held that assessments are made in favour of injured parties, creditors and women claiming under their marriage contracts (M Gittin V 1), and only land and not chattels could be included in such assessments.

With regard to chattels the rule remained that a person could take the law into his own hands, and *whoever comes first has a right to them;* there was only a proviso in favour of orphans who succeeded to such chattels (M Kethuboth IX 3). Later on it was held that "a person who lent to another should not make an attachment except through court" (M Baba Meṣia IX 3), which meant that prior authority of the court must be applied for, before seizure of the debtor's chattels. But the seizure was originally effected by the creditor himself : "if he behaves unashamedly in the matter of payment, one may not enter his house to make an attachment before the matter has been heard in court".[2] Only at a later stage was it held that the messenger of the court should go to seize the security from the debtor (TB Baba Meṣia 113b); and the creditor could no longer do so himself.[3]

2. LAWS AND JUDGE

The halakha did not classify laws according to the person who might eventually invoke them, and thus the division into private and public law is foreign to the halakha.[4] Laws were instead classified in accordance with the passage in the Torah, according to which the judge was called upon to consider the case; thus, terms such as *the law of the false-prophet* or *the law of the idolatrous city* (M Sanhedrin XI 5, X 4-6), *instruction* (T Horayoth I 3) and *sanctification of the new*

---

[1] For collection procedure in Hellenistic law see : Wolff, Beiträge, 110; Wolff, Justizwesen, 38; Taubenschlag Law, 208; Weiss, GPR, 465.

[2] Josephus, Antiquities, IV 8.26.268.

[3] Cf. Gulak, Obligations, 127; as to the messenger of the court in Hellenistic Law see : S. Plodzien, JJP V (1951) 217-27; Cl. Préaux, Chronique d'Egypte XXX (1955) 107-11.

[4] For the distinction between public and private law in the Greek system : Jones, Law 116 ff.

month (T Sanhedrin V 2) were used to denote the matters reserved for the jurisdiction of the 71-member Sanhedrin. Each case under these laws was apparently opened by the head of the court, that is to say by the High Priest or by the Prince, after witnesses had appeared before him and testified in the matter. In this regard such laws may be termed public.

Another group of laws stood midway between public and private action, since the court would become seized of cases under them through the testimony of an individual, though not necessarily through an individual's claim. Among such laws we find the *laws of capital cases* (M Sanhedrin I 4, IV 1),[1] under which the accused was liable to the penalty of death, and likewise *strokes* (M Sanhedrin I 2), laws under which the penalty provided was whipping.The laws most commonly invoked were *laws of moneys* (*civil cases*) M Sanhedrin I 1), prominent among which were *admissions and loans* (TB Sanhedrin 2b), which regulate relationships between individuals in matters of property. The plaintiff in such cases claims certain property or payment due him from the defendant. *Laws of monies* do not as a rule include *conversions* and *physical injuries ... full compensation, half compensation, double, four-fold and five-fold payments ... the ravisher, the seducer, the slanderer of a virgin"* (M Sanhedrin I 1). Such cases are governed by special passages in the Torah, and part of them are included in the *law of fines*(T Mo'ed Qatan II 11).[2] A separate framework comprises matters such as *loosening the shoe* (to avoid levirate marriage) and *refusals* (of a girl to marry according to her brother's decision, upon attaining majority) and *assessments* (M Sanhedrin I 3), which relate to the sanctity of the family or to Temple property. On the other hand, matters of betrothal and divorce and permission to marry were not counted as a class of cases, perhaps because they rarely came to court.

Rules of procedure probably first became definite in capital matters, and only later, and in a more limited way, in civil cases. The purpose of criminal procedure was to ensure leniency to the defendant : "and judge all men charitably" (M Aboth I 6), and these rules apparently came into being initially as a reaction to the severity of the Sadducee judges in the time of Alexander Jannaeus. The Mishna, in Sanhedrin, from the fourth capter on, preserves a collection of

---

[1] Cf. the Accadian term *din napishtim* in the Code of Hammurabi, 3, and its contrast *she'um u kaspum* (corn and money), *ibid.* parallel to Hebrew *laws of moneys*.

[2] However in both the Jerusalem and the Babylonian Talmuds the expression *strokes* is used in this context instead of *fines*.

rules of procedure in *capital cases*. The third chapter is a parallel collection related to *laws of moneys*.

Since the adjudication of civil cases was mostly in the hands of arbitrators or of local judges, it was in this field that the need first arose to define, who could be disqualified to judge or be witness (M Sanhedrin III 1-5). For capital cases permanent judges were appointed from among the prominent families (M Sanhedrin IV 2), and it was inconceivable that such a judge could be other than qualified. The rules were finally given wider effect when it was held that "anyone qualified to try capital cases is qualified to try civil cases, but there can be one who is capable of trying civil cases and is not capable of trying capital cases" (M Niddah VI 4).[1]

3. PARTIES AND TRIAL

Any person might apply to court to have his suit tried, regardless of whether both parties were men or "a man with a woman, or a woman with a man, or two women with each other" (Sifre Shofetim 190, TB Shebu'oth 30a). This rule of halakha is remarkable, since women were not competent to be either witness or judge and did not usually speak in a public forum. A slave could also sue, and it was only said that "it is bad to have any conflict with a slave or a women : anyone who injures them is liable wheras if they injure anyone they are exempt (M Baba Kama VIII 4), and the idea that they might need a guardian *ad litem* never arises. At times there were foreigners who took their cases before Jewish judges, and certain doubts were expressed as to the law to be applied in such cases (TB Baba Kama 113a).

Deaf-mutes, idiots and minors could sue, but it was held that "no oath need be taken as against the claim of a deaf-mute, an idiot or a minor, and no oath may be administered to a minor" (M Shebu'oth VI 4). This passage apparently deals with suits presented by a guardian in their behalf, and indeed such a suit requires the approval of the court, so that the rights of the deaf-mute, idiot and minor should not be prejudiced : "No case may be tried either against or on behalf

---

[1] For eligibility of judges see J. Ostrow, JQR XLVIII (1958), 359 ff.

of orphans, either to their gain or to their loss, unless permission has been obtained from court" (T Terumoth I 11).[1]

Although each party would generally argue for himself, the appearance of lawyers was not unknown. Indications of their functioning are first found in descriptions of the celestial court, in which there appears "an angel, an intercessor... to vouch for man's uprightness; Then he is gracious unto him, and saith : 'Deliver him from going down to the pit, I have found a ransom'" (Job XXXIII 23-24) and the Aramaic translation renders intercessor *paracleta*, derived from the Greek *parakletos*. The parable of the advocate arguing the innocence of Man before God is later on found in the book of Enoch (Ethiopic IX 3, XLIX 2-3, LXVIII 4), and it can only be understood in the light of commonly known activity of advocates in courts on earth.[2]

The parable found favour with the Sages also : "He who performs a commandment acquires an advocate, and he who commits a sin acquires a prosecutor" (M Aboth IV 11); and they described the argument between the advocate and the persecutor before the Divine throne. Indeed, the rule of procedure according to the halakha, and especially he rules of dependability and evidence were not adapted to the appearance of arguers learned in the law. Such arguers would show their clients how to argue on points of dependability, and thus bring the judges to decide in their favour. For this reason the Sages received the activity of lawyers with disfavour, saying : "Keep thee far from a false matter—do not appoint *advocates* to stand by you" (Mekhiltha d'R. Ishmael, Kaspa III). Accordingly the passage in Ezekiel XVIII 18, "and did that which is not good among his people", was expounded to mean "he who appears with a *power of attorney*" (TB Shebu'oth 31a).[3]

The suit was opened by application to the court to summon the defendant to attend trial in court.[4]

---

[1] Regarding parties who may sue under Greek law see : Lipsius, 789 ff.; Weiss, GPR, 164 ff.; Seidl, PtRG, 88.

[2] As to the advocate in the Divine court see : O. Betz, Der Paraklet, Leiden 1963; M. Miguens, El Paràclito, Jerusalem 1963; R. E. Brown, New Testament Studies XIII (1967) 113-32. As to advocates in Greek and Hellenistic Law : L. Wenger, Die Stellvertretung im Rechte der Papyri, Leipzig 1906, 122 ff; Latte-Seidl, *Synegoros*, R.E, IX, 1932, 1353 ff.; Taubenschlag, Law, 233 f.; R. Taubenschlag, F. Schulz Festschrift, Weimar 1951, II 188 ff.; Jones, Law, 143 ff.; Seidl, PtRG 88.

[3] Other terms for advocates are *entoleus* (apparently in money matters) and *antidikos*, the opponent's advocate.

[4] As to opening of a suit in Greek law : Lipsius, 804 ff.; E. Bernecker, Zur Geschichte der Prozesseinleitung im Ptolemäischen Recht, Ansbach 1930; Seidl PtRG, 85, 89 f.

An example is furnished in the story of Susanna, describing the procedure on a charge of adultery : "And the two elders, the judges, stood up and said : send and call Susanna the daughter of Ḥilkiah, the wife of Jehoiakim, and they called her forthwith". Similar to this is the opening of the case against the young Herod for having killed Hezekiah of Galilee and his comrades. The families of the victims applied to the king, charging that Herod must be brought to book before Hyrcanus according to the ancestral law, which forbids putting people to death without trial".[1] On the bases of this demand the king laid a charge against Herod.[2] In a similar narrative in TB Sanhedrin 19a it is said that the complaint was presented to the head of the Sanhedrin, and he said to his colleagues regarding the accused (King Jannaeus) : "Look well at him and we will try him. So they sent (a message to the king) : Your servant has killed a person...".[3] The summons was apparently made out in writing according to prescribed form, and it was called a message or a *diatagma* (i.e. an order) (TJ Qiddushin 70a).

When presenting his complaint, or soon afterwards the plaintiff sometimes presented a bill of arguments, like that indicated in Job XXXI 35 : "the indictment which mine adversary hath written". Such a statement of claim was apparently written at the dictation of the plaintiff by a scribe according to a certain form. In two statements of claim written in Greek in 218 B.C.E. Jews were brought to trial before the king of Egypt,[4] and perhaps such documents were drafted similarly in Judea. This statement of complaint was called an *enklema* (Deut. Rabba. II), and in Philo's description of the procedure in respect of an unfaithful wife, the husband is supposed to write a statement of claim : *grapsamenos proklesin*.[5]

On receipt of the statement of claim it was apparently recorded by the *scribes of the judges*,[6] and it was perhaps this practice which the

---

[1] Josephus, War I 10. 6. 209; Antiquities XIV 9. 4. 168. What the family asked of Hyrcanus was "that Herod be put on trial before the Sanhedrin for his acts".

[2] War, *ibid.*; in Antiquities, *ibid.*, it is related that the king "summoned Herod to come and give an account for the acts of which he was accused", meaning that he should appear before the Sanhedrin.

[3] In case this passage is identified with the story of Herod, and thus Hyrcanus is substituted for Jannaeus and Shmaiah or Shammai is substituted from Simon b. Shetaḥ, the Talmud wishes to describe the king as accused and Herod as his servant.

[4] CPJ, I, 128, 129. As to written statements of complaint in Greek and Hellenistic law : Lipsius, 815 ff.; Seidl, PtRG 85, 89 f.

[5] Laws III 10.53; and cf. Mantel, Sanhedrin, 312.

[6] Cf. Lipsius 820.

apocalyptic writings meant when they said that the guilt of a person was *recorded in heaven* (Enoch-Ethiopic LXXXI 4, XCVIII 7, CIV 7, Slavonic XIII 104; II Baruch XXIV 1; IV Ezra IV 20).

But recording in court could also apply to the pleadings before the judges or to the discussions of the judges among themselves. According to M Sanhedrin IV 3 : "two scribes of the judges stand before them ... and write the words of those who would acquit and of those who would convict", but it is possible that the record of the court also included the main points of the charge.

The existence of written court transcripts or judgments quite likely began at an early period, and is testified to by the many scriptural passages about a Divine book in which judgment passed on men is recorded (Ex. XXXII 32; Isaiah IV 3, LXV 6; Malachi III 16; Psalms LXIX 29, LXXXIX 16; Daniel VII 10; and also M Aboth II 1). This idea resembles that of the tablets of fate (*dupshunati*) in Babylonian texts, and must be an echo of the custom in the ordinary courts. It is of interest that the passage in Daniel X 21, "that which is inscribed in the writing of truth", is expounded by Gen. Rabba 81 to include both transcript and judgment : "inscribed—*before sentence*, truth—*after sentence has been pronounced*".

The book of the *living and the dead* and the book of *good and evil deeds* are frequently mentioned in the apocalyptic writings : "and behold there he writes down the condemnation and judgment of the world, and all the wickedness of the children of men" (Jubilees IV 23); "And the judgment of all is ordained and written on the heavenly tablets in righteousness—even (the judgment of) all who depart from the path which is ordained for them to walk in ... judgment is written down for every creature and for every kind (*ibid*. V 13-14); "I saw the Head of Days when He seated himself upon the throne of this glory, and the books of the living were opened before Him" (Enoch, Ethiopic XLVII 3-4); "For on the great Day of Judgment every act of man shall be recalled in writing" (Enoch, Slavonic XIII 52).[1]

Thus also in the thinking of the Sages : "All men are judged on the New Year and their *sentence is sealed* on the Day of Atonement" (T Rosh Hashana I 13), and the *books are opened* on the New Year (TB Rosh Hashana 16b). During the talmudic period the arguments

---

[1] Cf. : L. Koep, Das himmlische Buch in Antike und Christentum (Theophaneia, Beiträge zur Religions- und Kirchengeschichte, 8), Bonn 1952, 17 f.; *idem. s.v.* Buch, Reallexikon für Antike und Christentum II, 725 f.; as to court minutes and judgments in the Ptolemaic kingdom see CPJ 19.

of the parties were not recorded, but only the words of the judges
(M Sanhedrin IV 3), and therefore the parties were allowed to change
their arguments and raise new ones (TB Baba Bathra 31a).[1] Only in
bills of arbitration, when the parties agreed to submit to arbitration,
were their arguments included.

Proceedings were oral, so that the judges could be impressed by the
arguments of the parties, just as they were supposed to hear the
witnesses "from their own mouth and not from the mouth of their
writing". Therefore many rules of halakha were expressed in relation
to cases where "he says and she says", or "the one says and the other
says". Arguments generally refer to matters of fact and not of law,
and only after the witnesses have been heard would the judges speak
"first *for aquittal*" (M Sanhedrin V 4) then *for conviction* (M Sanhedrin
IV 1), after they had "discussed the matter".

If the parties were versed in halakha, or were represented by advocates, they would do more than merely describe the facts. As a consequence of such cases there came into being concise arguments based
on halakha as already determined in practice on a previous occasion.
An example of this can be seen in a case of husband and wife : "If a man
marries a woman and finds her not a virgin, she says : I was ravished
after you betrothed me so it was *your field that was flooded*, and he says :
Not so, but it happened before I betrothed you and it was *a mistaken
purchase*" (M Kethuboth I 6). Besides the statement of facts, each
party relies on a concise argument taken from civil law, and raised in
this context by way of analogy. The wife refers to the case where land
was let or mortgaged and the river swept away its harvest, and the
occupier may argue that the loss should fall on the owner : "if a man
makes his field security for his wife's rights under her marriage contract, and it is flooded by a river, she may collect from other property"
(T Kethuboth XI 8). On the other hand the husband refers to the law
under which a purchaser may retract if the vendor has deceived him,
as "if a man sells wine to another and it turns sour ... and if it is
known that his wine goes sour—it is *a mistaken purchase*" (M Baba
Bathra VI 3).

A similar argument is *here is your property in front of you*, used
both in cases of conversion (M Baba Kama IX 2, X 5) and of rental
(M Baba Meṣia VI 3). The circumstances in which such an argument is

---

[1] As long as the new argumentation could be reconciled with the previous one.

used are quite different in the two sets of cases,[1] and this example illustrates the inventiveness of the parties in extending the application of an argument beyond its original limits.

Similarly the parties present arguments based on logic, especially in civil cases. Two examples are brought by Admon, most likely based on his experience of cases heard by him as a *judge of decrees* : "He may say : if I owed you anything you should have collected when you sold me the field", or "if I really owe you anything, why are you borrowing from me" (M Kethuboth XIII 8, 9).

No express rule of halakha from early days has been preserved in which the court is warned "not to hear one party before the other party is present" (TB Sanhedrin 7b), but this important principle may be assumed to have been accepted during the Second Commonwealth.[2] The principle of open trial was certainly taken for granted,[3] especially in courts composed of many judges, such as the Great and Small Sanhedrin. Public trial of capital cases was required so as to enable anybody who would testify for the defence to know about the case and come forward; for the same reason moreover, the judgment itself would be announced by a crier (M Sanhedrin VI 1). And in the case of collection of money out of the proceed of property of orphans, announcement was made in public, so as to ensure that the highest possible price is received (Arakhin VI 1).[4]

In M Sanhedrin IV 1 some of the rules of procedure are preserved : "Civil cases may be decided on the same day, whether the finding is for or against the defendant; capital cases may be decided on the same day in favour of the defendant, and (only) on the next day against him. Therefore trial may not open on the day before the Sabbath or a Holiday". These rules, as is known, were not observed in the trial of Jesus, and if the Gospels are to be relied on, the rule was not followed because Jesus was accused of enticing and drawing away (see Deut. XIII 7-12; T Sanhedrin X 11).[5]

Another rule of halakha for civil cases is this : "How do they try

[1] Cf. Albeck, Mishna, Addenda *ad loc.*

[2] For this principle see : Seidl, PtRG 85; Kaser, RZPR, 9.

[3] See : Seidl, PtRG 87; Kaser, RZPR, 9.

[4] Cf. infra, p. 111.

[5] For recent literature on the trial of Jesus see : H. Cohn, The Trial and Death of Jesus of Nazareth (Hebrew), Tel Aviv 1968; I. Baer, Zion (Hebrew) XXXI (1966) 135-145, and bibliography listed. As to the duty in Greek law to conclude trial on the same day, see Lipsius, 911 ff.

cases ? The judges sit and the parties stand before them, and the one who sues another opens his case first" (T Sanhedrin VI 3).

4. JUDGMENT

Immediately after hearing evidence the judges would *discuss the matter* (M Sanhedrin III 6), that is so to say they would deal with the facts and the law of the case in order to draw out the arguments for and against the defendant. In capital cases the first speaker would be one in his favour : "they *open in his favour* and not against him" (M Sanhedrin IV 1), and even a witness or a disciple may argue in favour of the accused, and of course the accused could have his say. The discussion of the judges was held in the presence of the public (M Sanhedrin V 4). "The scribes of the judges stand before them ... and write down the words of those who hold in favour of the accused and of those who hold against him" (M Sanhedrin IV 3), and in "capital cases—one who holds against the accused may hold in his favour but one who holds in his favour may not retract and hold against him" (M Sanhedrin IV 1).

If the judges were not unanimous they would *stand up to be counted* (M Sanhedrin V 5), and in capital cases they would *start from the side* (M Sanhedrin IV 2) so that a junior judge at the side of the *circular half threshing floor* need not hesitate to differ from his senior.[1] The decision would be that of the majority, but "in civil cases a majority of one decides, whether for or against the defendant, and in capital cases a majority of one decides in his favour and (only) a majority of two may decide against him" (M Sanhedrin IV 1).[2] When there is a middle way possible, as in assessment of property for purposes of collecting a debt, such a way is followed : "Where three people enter property to assess it, and one assesses it at one hundred and two at two hundred—the opinion of the one is of no value, as he is a minority; if one assesses it at one hundred, one at twenty (selas=eighty dinars), and one at thirty (selas=one hundred and twenty dinars), it is considered as being one hundred" (TB Baba Bathra 107a).

It should be noted that when a decision was made by a majority,

---

[1] While the vote was taken everybody else was excluded from the place; "when the matter was finished, they would be allowed in" (M Sanhedrin III 7).

[2] As to the dictum "if the Sanhedrin is unanimous for conviction he is acquitted" (TB Sanhedrin 17a) see E. E. Halevi, Tarbiz (Hebrew) XXXVI (1967) 90.

it is not said that *the majority is like the whole* (TB Horayoth 3b), but that *the majority is followed* (T Horayoth I 3), and the decision is that of the majority only. Hence certain sages came to consider the count to include only those voting for the decision, and therefore "civil cases, Rabbi (Judah the Prince) says : by five (judges), *so that judgment may be given by three*" (T Sanhedrin I 1). In this way one can interpret the Mishna that holds that "no court may annul the words of another court unless it is *greater in wisdom and in number*" (M Eduyoth I 5). This passage deals with the Great Sanhedrin, whose number is fixed at seventy-one, and the *number* may refer to the number of sages who voted for a certain statute, a number which may be subject to change.[1] With the passage of time the principle was accepted that *the majority is like the whole* and the count was taken to include all the judges, even if some of them voted against the decision. This was the meaning of the term count in the context of sanctification of months and declaring leap years : "and they decide by seven, as there is no count less than seven" (T Sanhedrin II 1).

The judge *acquits* the party or *condemns* him, and thus the party is *zakkai* (innocent) or *ḥayyab* (condemned) (M Sanhedrin III 7, V 5), in civil as well as in capital cases. The primary meanung of *zakkai* and *ḥayyab* is righteous and wicked (Deut. XXV 1). In M Aboth I 8 judges are thus exhorted : " And when the parties to a suit are standing before you, let them both be regarded by you as wicked, but when they are departed from your presence, regard them both as innocent".[2]

Although judgment has been pronounced, the judges may retract and the loosing party may sue again : "in civil cases (judgment) may be retracted, whether to acquit or to condemn; in capital cases—only to acquit and not to condemn" (M Sanhedrin IV 1). Even in the stage of execution of the judgment it may be disproved : "When judgment has been given he is taken out to be stoned ...A man stands at the door of the court and the shawls are in his hand, and another rides on a horse at a distance from him so as to be seen by him. If anyone says, I have something to say in his favour, the man with the shawls waves and the horseman rushes and stops him; even if he

---

[1] Cf. Maimonides, Hilkhoth Mamrim II 2; Albeck, Mishna Addenda *ad loc.*

[2] *Zakkai* and its derivatives, in time, took on, in addition to the original meaning of innocence declared by court, the meaning of any right asserted, either by operation of law or under contract. Thus they are used in contexts such as these : "Whoever comes first *acquires* them" (M Kethuboth VIII 7); "He lost his right" (M Kethuboth XIII 6); "I *acquired* it" (M Baba Meṣia I 3).

himself says, I have something to say in my favour, he is brought
back, even a fourth and fifth time, as long as there is substance to
his words. If they find reason to acquit him—they release him; if
not—he goes out to be stoned" (M Sanhedrin VI 1). The same rule
applies in civil cases : "at any time he brings evidence he may disprove
the judgment" (M Sanhedrin III 8).[1]

In order to keep proceedings within bounds, it was apparently the
practice to oblige the judgment debtor to write a bill in favour of the
judgment creditor, to the effect that he will raise no further litigation
in connection with the subject-matter of the suit. Such bills are termed
deeds of renunciation in the bills of Elephantine;[2] and an indication
of such a formula appears in M Kethuboth IX 1. *Bills of admission*
were an outgrowth of this formula, calculated as they were to preclude denial of the facts once decided between the parties. By writing
such a bill, the judgment became *res judicata* and irrefutable.

A technique similar to that of the deed of renunciation was for the
court to "say to him, any (further) evidence that you have—bring
within thirty days from today; if he finds within thirty days, he may
disprove; if not, he may not disprove" (M Sanhedrin III 8). Although
Rabban Simon b. Gamliel held this rule to be unlawful (*ibid.*), it may
be assumed that the rule was in common use, *ut sit finis litium*.

In the wake of these practices an idea similar to that of *res judicata*
was adopted, so much so that it was held : "If he tried a case and
found the wrong party in the right or the right party in the wrong,
or the pure impure or the impure pure— what he did *is done*, and he
shall pay from his own house" (M Bekhoroth IV 4).[3]

Even in capital cases, where the witnesses would retract their
evidence and thus disprove the judgment, the doctrine of finality
obtains : "In a certain case a man was being taken out to be stoned
and they said to him, confess; he said, may my death atone for all
my sins and if I did this may it not be forgiven me, and may the court
of Israel be guiltless. And when he was brought before the Sages,
tears flowed from their eyes. They said to them it is *impossible to*

---

[1] Regarding *res judicata* in Greek law see : E. Berneker, Festschrift, P. Koschaker,
III (1939) 268-80; E. Berneker, JJP IV (1950) 253-64; R. Taubenschlag, Opera Minora,
Warsaw 1959, II, 703; Seidl, PtRG, 99.

[2] Yaron, Introduction, 33, 75, 81.

[3] This rule does, indeed, assume that action may be taken against a judge who was
in error, and that he might be obliged personally to pay. But as far as the opposing
party is concerned the litigation is closed.

revoke the trial, and there is no end to the matter, but his blood will hang from the neck of his witnesses" (T Sanhedrin IX 5).[1]

5. EXECUTION

We have already mentioned the procedure of collection of promissory notes as evidenced by two Aramaic documents from the fifth century B.C.E. in Elephantine, Egypt.[2] The borrower promises the lender, at the time the money changes hands, that he may *take for himself* any securities that he finds in the house, even after the borrower's death. There is indeed no mention of a right to collect, and the documents speak only of the right to demand pledge from the debtor,[3] but in practice this is a way to collect without the help of the court, especially as the borrower declares that he will be unable to complain in court of the act of the lender : "nor shall I have power to lodge a complaint against you before governor or judge on the ground that you have taken from me any security while this deed is in your hand".[4]

The liability of property was generally included in New Babylonian bills,[5] and from there it apparently penetrated the customary forms of the scribes in Palestine. The debtor would write in the promissory note "all my property is *liable*" for the said debt, and Simon b. Shetaḥ included the condition in the common form of marriage contract (T Kethuboth XII 1, TB Kethuboth 82b, TJ *ibid*. VIII 11. 32b). Under such a clause the lender is given title to the property of the debtor from the time the borrower receives the loan, and he could accordingly collect his debt, apparently without recourse to court. The ancient form of such liability applied only to such property as existed at the time the debt was created, as Simon b. Shetaḥ enacted : "All property *that I have* is responsible and liable for this thy Kethuba" (T Kethuboth XII 1). On the other hand, the Demotic writers of

---

[1] Rashi on Sanhedrin 44b ascribes the incident to the son of Simon b. Shetaḥ, following TJ Sanhedrin VI 5, 23b.

[2] Regarding collection of debts in Greece and Egypt see : Taubenschlag, Law, 524 ff.; Weiss, GPR, 451-543; Seidl, PtRG, 100 ff.

[3] Yaron, Introduction, 96 f.; Cowley, AP, 10; Kraeling, AP, 11.

[4] By contrast, Seidl, PtRG. assumes that the formula in the Greek bill did not allow collection except by court process. Regarding this formula see also H. Kupizewski, Eos XLVIII, 3 (1957) (=Symbolae R. Taubenschlag) 89-103; Wolff, Beiträge, 102-128.

[5] See Tarbiz (Hebrew) XXXVII (1968) 43.

bills in Egypt would add a *floating charge* on the property the debtor
might thereafter acquire; from there the technique reached Palestine
and it appears in the bills of Murabba'at : "Payment shall be effected
to you from my property, and from *whatever I shall acquire* you shall
have the right of seizure" (DJD II 101).[1]

The liability clause refers to property, and it cannot be decided
whether the term means real property only or whether it includes
chattels as well. The main significance of the clause is in regard to
real property, as it enables it to be subject to a charge without being
delivered to the creditor. Chattels, on the other hand, could be deposited
with the lender upon receipt of the loan money, and then no bill would
be necessary.

Therefore property liability came to refer to real property only,
and the term *property having liability* would denote real property and
property that has no liability would denote chattels (M Qiddushin
I 5). It is possible, however, that real property was called *property that
has liability* because the seller would undertake to defend the purchaser's title, and thus to be liable for the sale in case anyone with a
claim to better title, or a creditor of the seller, seizes the sold property
from the purchaser. Such liability would not be furnished in sale of
chattels and perhaps that is why they are termed *property that has
no liability*. In either case, liability runs with real property only.[2]

The main purpose of property liability is to continue in effect even
after the debtor sells the property to someone else, thus : "A person who
makes a loan to another upon a bill may collect from *charged property*
(M Baba Bathra X 8). How the contrary term, *free property*, came into
use meaning real property in the possession of the debtor at the time
of collection, is a matter which requires explanation. It appears to me
that *charged property* is mainly that from which a debt may be collected
even if the property has been sold, since it was charged in a promissory
note. Free property is that which was not so charged, and thus from
which a debt may be collected only if in the possession of the debtor
but not if alienated. Thus, property that remained in the debtor's
possession came to be termed *free property*, whether or not a bill
of liability was written.[3]

The Aramaic bill found in Elephantine, as we have seen, allowed

---

[1] Cf. Tarbiz (Hebrew) XXXII (1963) 20[3]; Yaron, JJS XI (1960) 166; and see Gulak,
Obligation, 39.

[2] Cf. Gulak, Obligation, 32 ff.

[3] Cf. Gulak, Obligation, 34.

the creditor to take chattels of the debtor as security until the debt
would be paid. A person could *lend upon a pledge* taking his pledge
when making the loan;[1] similarly, the borrower could *mortgage* a house
to him or *mortgage* a field to him", delivering the property to the
possession of the lender at the time the loan is made. However, the
borrower could also make certain property an *hypotheke* at the time
the loan was made, under which arrangement he would allow the lender,
in case the debt is not paid when due, to collect the debt by seizure
of the property.[2]

From here we come to collection under extra-contractual provisions :
under legal rights and by court order. Collection proceedings which
included attachment of the debtor's property were first created in the
Temple. The treasurer's agents would go around and *take pledges*
from the debtors (M Shekalim I 3, VII 5; Arakhin V 6), and if they
found no property they used other means to exact payment. Thus it
was said : "Woe to us from the house of Ishmael b. Piabi, for they
are high priests and their sons are treasurers and their sons-in-law
are overseers, and their servants come and beat us with sticks" (T
Menaḥoth XIII 21).

On the other hand, the agents would, in considering the needs of
the debtor, "leave him food for thirty days, clothing for twelve months,
a made bed, and sandals and phylacteries ... If he was an artisan they
would leave him two of each kind of tool of his trade ..." (M Arakhin
VI 3; T Arakhin IV 6).[3]

As indicated above, it is probable that the courts began to deal
with collection of debts out of real property, whereas collection from
chattels remained the right of the lender. Even in regard to real
property the courts did consider it his right to deal with actual
collection; originally they only required that the creditor notify them,

---

[1] Cf. *op. cit.* 62 ff.

[2] Cf., *op. cit.*, 53 ff.

[3] R. Elizer later added rules in the benefit of farmers and mule-drivers (*ibid.*). Such
rules were created by exegesis of Ex. XXII 25-26 and Deut. XXIV 6, 10-13, 17. Similar
rules were issued by Ptolemy Euergetes II in the year 118 B.C.E.: A.S. Hunt & C.C
Edgar Select Papyri II (Loeb Classical Library), London 1934, No. 210; Seidl, PtRG,
104. These rules, originally applying to the Temple, were later extended to apply to lay
creditors : "he may not take from him as a pledge anything with which food is made,
and he must leave a bed and bed and mattress for a rich man, a bed and bed and mat
for a poor man ..." (TB Baba Meṣia 113b), and cf. the amended version *ibid. :* "the same
arrangement left in case of assessed vows for the Temple is left in case of a creditor.
And cf. Gulak, Obligation 134 ff.

and on the grounds of such notice they would authorise him to collect his debt from the debtor's property. Regarding such authority they perhaps first became strict in cases where the creditor wished to collect from charged property, for the third party who bought it would of course oppose the creditor's taking of the law into his own hands.

The *prosbolé* [1] was known in Jewish law even before Hillel's time : it was a mere formal notice by the lender of intention to collect. After the creditor gave such notice, collection proceedings begun, the seventh year would not release, and the borrower could not complain that the lender was taking the law into his own hands.

Meanwhile a certain order was prescribed for collection of debts for the Temple : to ensure that real property above the value of the debt would not be seized, the property would first be *assessed : "Assessment* of dedicated property would last sixty days, with announcements every morning and evening" (M Arakhin VI 1). Such *assessment* was thus a public auction which lasted for months to enable the tenders to be examined. It was similarly held (*ibid.*) that "*assessment* of orphans' property would last thirty days", meaning that the court must determine the value of the property by means of auction, before the creditor could seize it for his debt (M Kethuboth XI 5). In this way there came to be one rule for injured parties, creditors and women collecting under marriage contract : all of them had to go through the procedure of assessment before they could collect what was due to them (M Gittin V 1), and the assessment would be recorded in a writ of court, termed as *letter of assessment* (M Baba Meşia I 8). [2]

---

[1] Cf. *supra* p. 22, regarding fiction. As to the term see L. Blau, Festschrift zum 50-jährigen Bestehen der Landesrabbinerschule, Budapest 1927; S. Zeitlin, JQR XXXVII (1946-7) 341-62; M. Ginsburg, Arctos III (1962) 37-44.

[2] See Gulak, Obligation, 118; Weiss, GPR, 465; Wolff, Beiträge, 110; and *supra*. The procedure of assessment existed already during the Second Commonwealth, and after the destruction the question arose : "If three people inspect property to assess it, one assesses at one hundred and two assess at two hundred ... R. Elazar b. R. Zadok says ... (T Kethuboth XI 2). As to auction procedures and direct execution by the creditor, and as to supervision imposed by the State in such matters see : Weiss, GPR 451 ff.; F. Pringsheim Gesammelte Abhandlungen, Heidelberg 1961, II, 267.

CHAPTER FIVE

EVIDENCE

1. SUPERNATURAL EVIDENCE

Superhuman proof was relied upon, in certain matters, by judges in the Second Commonwealth.[1] The most important of these matters is that of the woman suspected of adultery and the administration of bitter water to her as described in Mishna Sotah. It is recorded that there was "a case of a Carchemite emancipated slave-woman in Jerusalem, to whom Shma'ya ad Abtalion administered the water", (M Eduyoth V 6). At the end of this period it was told of Queen Helene who came from Adiabene and became a proselyte together with her son King Monbaz, that "she made a tablet of gold, on which there was written the passage dealing with the woman suspected of adultery" (M Yoma III 10). However it became realized that in most cases this was not the best way to arrive at the truth, and it was therefore held : "If she had any merit—it would delay the punishment. Merit may suspend the punishment for one year, for two years, or for three years" (M Sotah III 4). And in the days of Rabban Yoḥanan b. Zakkai it was said that "as adulterers have increased, bitter water has ceased" (M Sotah IX 9).[2]

Similarly, "the House of Hillel says, testimony may be given regarding a *divine voice*" (T Nazir I 1); "a case is reported of a person who stood at the summit of a mountain and said, 'X son of Y of the place Z has died'—and they went and found no one there, and they allowed his wife to remarry, and yet another case is been reported of a person in Ṣalmon who said, 'I, X son of Y', have been bitten by a snake, and I am now dead"—and they went and did not recognize him, yet they allowed his wife to remarry" (M Yebamoth XVI 6). However, "the House of Shammai says, no testimony may be given regarding a *divine voice*" (T Nazir I 1). Even after the Destruction the

---

[1] Regarding superhuman proof in Greek law see K. Latte, Heiliges Recht, Tübingen 1920; L. Gernet, Droit et Société dans la Grèce ancienne, Paris 1955, 9 ff., 62 ff.; Jones, Law, 136 f.; Recueils de Société Jean Bodin XVI (1965), 119 ff.

[2] And cf. Epstein, Tannaitic Lit. 41, and N. Wahrmann, Untersuchungen zur Stellung der Frau, Breslau 1933, and the review by M. Guttmann, MGWJ (1936) 425 ff.

divine voice was relied upon in deciding a dispute between the Houses
of Hillel and Shammai (TB Erubin 13b, TJ Yebamoth I *ad fin.*), and
this may be why the House of Shammai did not want to rely on a
divine voice.[1]

2. DEPENDABILITY

Dependability of arguments and of evidence could be either stipulated
between the parties or prescribed by law, but was not left to the judge.
As for the parties : in the promissory note the debtor could promise
that he would not object to seizure of property by the creditor, and
that the creditor's mere holding of the note would be conclusive
evidence of his right : "nor shall I have power to lodge complaint
against you before governor or judge on the ground that you have
taken from me any security while this deed is in your hand".[2] In a
conveyance the seller undertakes to raise no objection in the future
to the title of the buyer, and nullifies the effect of such an objection
in advance : "I shall have no power to institute suit or process against
you ... Whoever sues you in my name concerning this land will pay
you the sum of 20 karash royal weight and the land is assuredly yours".[3]

Such stipulations were common between husband and wife, and
perhaps in general between persons who made an agreement *on trust*,
such as the negotiator on trust : "A person who made a written promise
to his wife before marriage, *I shall have no right or claim* to your
property" (KethubothIX 1); "If he wrote, *I shall have no right to
demand of you* a vow or an oath" (M Kethuboth IX 5).[4]

Apparently, the duty to take an oath in order to dispel doubts,
imposed upon "partners, share-croppers, guardians, a wife in charge
of the house, and a co-heir" (M Shebu'oth VII 8), originally based on
agreement, later on became an implied term. Such an agreement, in
effect, ascribed *dependability* to the legal owner of the property,
even if he made no positive claim and brought no evidence. Its

---

[1] Regarding the law of evidence in the halakha see Z. Frankel, Der gerichtliche Beweis
nach mosaisch-talmudischem Recht, Berlin 1846; B. Cohen, Recueils de Société Jean
Bodin XVI (1965) 103 ff.; H. Jaeger, *ibid.*, 423 ff.

[2] Cowley, AP 10; Yaron, Introduction, 97.

[3] Cowley, AP 6; Yaron, Introduction, 86; see also DJD II 26, where Milik reads
"il sera sans effet légal (tout autre document) qu'on vous présentera" As to this clause
in Greek and Egyptian law see Seidl, PtRG, 93.

[4] Cf. Gulak, Urkundenwesen, 118, and T Baba Meṣia III 22.

effect ceased upon partition of the property, insofar as "if the partners or share-croppers have partitioned—he cannot impose an oath upon him" (M Shebu'oth VII 8), similarly, "if his guardianship has ceased he is like any other person" (T Kethuboth IX 3).

But in the main, *dependability* is derived from provisions of law which determine when a person's word may be conclusively accepted.[1] *Dependability* is of two kinds : that of a witness and that of a litigant. The *dependability* of a witness is a question that arises when there is the testimony of one witness only, or where witnesses testify to an unusual fact. A woman, keeper of an inn, testifying to the death of a person in order that his widow might remarry, was held to be *dependable* (M Yebamoth XVI 7). Similarly, witnesses may retract, or they may testify to things they saw when they were minors : these were considered instances of *dependability* (M Kethuboth II 3, 10).[2] In civil matters, a depositary a vendor and a judge are vested with *dependability* (T Baba Meṣia I 10-12).

The general rule is that "a person is not *dependable* regarding himself" (M Kethuboth II 9), but in matrimonial cases exceptions to the rule were allowed. Thus, a woman who came "from the harvest" and said her husband has died was *depended upon*—and was allowed to remarry (M Yebamoth XV 1-2), and women were *depended upon* in other cases, where the reasoning was that "the mouth that prohibited is the mouth that permitted" (M Kethuboth II 5, Eduyoth III 6). Similarly, a person was considered *dependable* regarding his wife and children (M Qiddushin III 7-8, Baba Bathra VIII 6).

Rules of *dependability* may have been originally created in matters of tithes and of purity. *Dependability* was then vested in a select group of pietists and was limited to matters of *prohibition and permission*. [3] "A person who undertakes to be a *trusted* person—tithes ... and does not lodge in the house of an unlearned person" (M Demai II 2).

---

[1] As to rules of dependability and the power of the judge to weigh evidence under Greek law see : W. Hellebrand, Das Prozesszeugnis im Rechte der gräko-ägyptischen Papyri (MB, 18), 1934, 173 ff., Seidl, PtRG, 96; and as to this problem in Roman law : G. Broggini, Coniectanea, Milano 1966, 146 n. 30, 167 ff.; Kaser, RZPR 8 f. Rules of *dependability* in the halakha are discussed by B. Kaatz, Jeshurun XV (1928), 89-98, 179-187.

[2] On the other hand the ordinary testimony of two witnesses did not involve the problem of *dependability* : the witnesses had only to pass examination. In this connection see the saying concerning fraudulent testimony, TB Shebu'oth 30b, indicating that the judge can refuse to try the case, but cannot declare the witnesses *undependable*.

[3] See *supra* p. 16. note 3.

Among such *trusted* persons the appellation *trusted* was used, thus
distinguishing them from the *unlearned persons*, who could not be
depended upon. These terms were adopted by the sages,[1] and, in
consequence, the judges could formulate concepts of *dependability*
in inter-human relationships as well.

On the other hand, the halakha ascribed absolute *dependability* to
two witnesses who passed examination in court,[2] and also to a person
who took the decisive oath imposed upon him. In such cases the
judge had no discretion to weigh the evidence or the oath and declare
them unreliable : he was in duty bound to give judgment according to
the legal rule. Thus, the sentence of death passed on the son of Simon
b. Shetaḥ remained valid, even though the witnesses admitted at
the end that their testimony was false (TJ Sanhedrin VI 5, 23b;
TB Sanhedrin 44b). Similarly the Law prescribes : "Wherever the
Torah imposes an oath the person taking the oath does not pay ...
These swear in order to collect : a person hired, a person from whom
a thing has been stolen, a person bodily injured, a person whose
opponent's oath would be suspect, and a store-keeper concerning
his account-book" (M Shebu'oth VII 1). [3]

3. Burden and Nature of Proof

In civil matters the rule prevails : "evidence must be brought by
the party wishing to take away from the other"; the rule is referred
to by Rabban Yoḥanan b. Zakkai (T Sotah XIII 10) and by R. Eliezer
(M Bikkurim II 10). It probably existed during the days of the Temple,
and a parallel rule is reported in the name of Judah b. Tabbai: "when
the parties to a suit are standing before you, regard them both as
wicked, but when they are departed from your presence, regard them
both as innocent, the verdict having been acquisced in by them"
(Aboth I 8). The parties here referred to are mainly parties to civil
suits, and therefore the judge should believe neither of them until
they support their claims by evidence. But even the losing party may
be justified if he undertakes to carry out the judgment.

---

[1] Similarly, some of the early Sages held a single witness to be *dependable* in matters
of prohibition, to enable a person to eat at another's table.

[2] Unless they were unqualified, see *infra*.

[3] See however TB Kethuboth 85a, showing that later on the judge was given discretion to demand an oath.

A similar presumption exists in *capital cases*, and perhaps also in cases involving *fines*. This is the context of the dictum of Joshua b. Peraḥya : "and judge all men charitably " (Aboth I 6). It is the origin of the Pharisee doctrine of leniency in justice and of seeking extenuating factors in the behavior of the accused person.[1]

Evidence would generally be brought through witnesses, the term evidence being synonymous with witnesses : "If a person says, give two hundred dinars to the people of my town ... and *evidence* may not be brought from the *people of that town*" (T Baba Bathra IX 9). Evidence may also mean other modes of proof, such as a bill : "If they said to him, bring *witnesses*, and he said, I have no witnesses, or they said to him, bring *evidence*, and he said, I have no evidence" (M Sanhedrin III 8).

It may be assumed that no clear distinction was made between factual evidence and legal argument, and evidence from Scripture might be submitted instead of evidence of happenings. This is a proper construction of M Baba Bathra VI 4 : in dealing with an agreement to build a house, the Mishna, instead of relying on local custom or on an implied term, says that "evidence in the matter is the Temple", that the contractor must build every house "to a height half its length and half its breadth".[2] It may be assumed that the chapters of the Mishna containing this rule are based upon precedents and legal customs, and thus this passage illustrates the character of evidence, such as could be brought in a concrete instance.[3]

A party could also adduce circumstantial evidence to support his claims. Examples of such evidence, taken from legal practice, were included in the halakha : "If a person presents a promissory note against a person, and that person presents a bill by which the former had sold him his field—Admon says : He may say, if I had owed you anything you should have collected what was due you when you sold me the field", or "If two people present promissory notes against each other—Admon says : If I owed you anything, how could you borrow from me ?" (M Kethuboth XIII 8-9).

---

[1] As to the burden of poof in Greek law—Jones, Law 275 f., and in Roman law—G. Pugliese, RIDA[3] III (1956) 349 ff.; G. Pugliese, Jura XI (1960) 149 ff.; Kaser, RZPR, *s.v. Beweislast*.

[2] The Greek rhetoricians also did not distinguish between factual evidence and legal arguments : Lipsius, 866 ff.; G. Pugliese, Recueils de Société Jean Bodin XVI (1965) 301, 308, 344.

[3] The interpretation given in the Mishna refers to a specific agreement; it was first voiced by the judge in an actual case.

Further : where "a woman became widowed or divorced, and says, I was virgin at marriage" evidence regarding the wedding may be brought, as to whether it was in the fashion of weddings of virgins (M Kethuboth II 1). And where a contract of sale has to be construed to determine the extent of the property sold, R. Judah allows circumstantial evidence : *"The money proves.* How ? If he said to him, sell me your pair for two hundred zuz—it is well known that the price of a pair is not two hundred zuz" (M Baba Bathra V 1).[1]

Such circumstantial evidence was admissible in civil cases; in capital cases only direct evidence was allowed. "Simon b. Shetaḥ said, May I see comfort [2] if I did not see a person running after another person into a ruin, and I ran after him, and I saw a sword in his hand and its blood dripping and the victim in the throes of death. And I said to him, you wicked man, who killed this person, I or you ? But what can I do, since your blood is not in my hands, as the Torah has said : 'At the mouth of two … witnesses shall he that is to die be put to death' (Deut XVII 6). May He who knows all thoughts punish the person who killed his fellow-man" (TB Sanhedrin 37b).

In other matters, on the other hand, rumours and public opinion are sometimes given consideration. Thus, for instance, a man may divorce his wife "because of *bad imputations*" (M Gittin IV 7), but "if *bad imputations* have circulated against a woman, the children are legitimate, as they are within the presumption of being the husband's" (T Yebamoth XII 8). Even in civil matters, notoriety may be used to clarify facts : "If a person recognizes his own things or books in the hands of someone else, and it is *well known in the town* that he has been stolen from—their purchaser shall swear to him how much he paid for them, and he shall take (the money and return the things), if it is not (well-known), his mere saying so is not sufficient, as I may say that he sold them to someone else and this man bought from that man" (M Baba Kama X 3).[3]

---

[1] Regarding circumstantial evidence in the halakha see A. Bakshi, Torah sh'be al-pe (Hebrew) X (1968) 135-143 ; H. Hefetz, Mishpatim (Hebrew) I (1968) 67-85.

[2] The intent of this expression is self-maledictory, similar to "may I lose my sons"; for if the comfort of Jerusalem were intended the expression would not be appropriate to Simon b. Shetaḥ.

[3] As to rumours in Roman law see : Digesta 22.5.3.2. ; 48.5.11.11 ; G. Broggini, Coniectanea, 173 ; G. Pugliese, Recueil de Société Jean Bodin XVI (1965) 340.

4. TESTIMONY

In the Bible the role of witnesses is not merely *probative*. They are called upon to give effect to solemn acts between persons. They take part in the conclusion of a covenant between two parties, in the redemption of a field in the transfer of title to land—not only in order to be able to give testimony later on, if a dispute arises, but also in order to give effect to the agreement itself.

On the other hand, Second Commonwealth halakha appears not to be familiar with the function of *constitutive* witnesses, but only with that of *probative* witnesses. In the chapter dealing with acquisitions no mention is made of witnesses present at the acquisition of either a wife or of property (M Qiddushin I 1-5). Only after the Destruction was a bill of divorcement held invalid *for lack of witnesses on it* (M Gittin IX 4), but yet it was held that "if she married the child is legitimate" (*ibid.*).[1]

Witnesses also acted as prosecutors and policemen. In the Story of Susanna, which in the Septuagint is appended to the Book of Daniel, the witnesses accuse the adulterous woman, and on the ground of their accusation she is required to attend trial by the community.[2]

The Sages required of witnesses that they should *caution* the accused immediately prior to the act constituting the offence, and they were therefore questioned in capital cases : "Did you *caution* him ?" (M Sanhedrin V 1). It was due to a tendency towards leniency that the halakha in the days of the Mishna required such *cautioning* : for when R. Akiba asked that mercy be exercised in regard to the children of the people of idolatrous cities, R. Eliezer replied that "even adults may not be put to death except if there were witnesses and *cautioning*" (T Sanhedrin XIV 3).[3]

It is unlikely that such a rule of halakha was in effect at the time when the courts dealt with capital cases, for no one would agree to

---

[1] Again, in M Yebamoth III 8 the divorce is in doubt but the bill is not invalid. However, these passages may be based on the assumption that "witnesses of delivery effect the divorce" (M Gittin IX 4), but under this rule itself the role of verifying witnesses as to the writing of the bill of divorcement is rendered insignificant.

[2] Regarding this story see N. Brüll, Jahrbuch für jüdische Geschichte und Literatur III (1877) 1-69; B. Revel, JQR III (1912-13) 344; J.D.M. Derrett, NTSt X (1963) 24 f.; J.M. Grinz, H. Albeck Jubilee Volume (Hebrew), Jerusalem, 1963, 150.

[3] As to the rule regarding *cautioning*, see P. Daykan, Sinai (Hebrew) L (1967) 51-62; Z. Karel, Bitzaron (Hebrew) XXII (1950) 110; Ch Rabin, QS, 110.

risk the penalty of death by expressly disregarding a *caution*. It may therefore be presumed that the rule regarding *cautioning* during the Second Commonwealth resembled the concept of *previous conviction* in modern criminal law, indicating that in regard to certain offences the accused would be convicted only if he repeated the offence.

The Torah, on two occasions, provides for increased severity of punishment due to *previous conviction*. In Deut XXI 18-19, in the passage dealing with the stubborn and rebellious son, the wording is "and though they chasten him (he) will not hearken into them, then shall his father and his mother lay hold on him, and bring him out unto the elders of his city". This was interpreted by the Sages to say that "he is to be *cautioned* in front of a court of three and to be whipped. If he repeats his offence he is to be tried by (a court of) twenty-three" (M Sanhedrin VIII 4). Thus the law requires *cautioning* in the case of a stubborn and rebellious son, and such *cautioning* is counted as a conviction as well, not only witnesses were present but also a court.

In the case of a goring ox, again, the Torah distinguishes between a first offender, as it were, and a *warned* ox (Ex. XXI 28-29, 35-36), and the Sages again explain, "And warning has been given to its owner—indicating that he is not liable unless *warned*" (Mekhiltha d' R. Ishmael *ad loc.*). In this context it is evident that instead of the biblical verb *hu'ad*, derived from the same root as *'ed*, meaning witness, the Sages use the verb *huthra*, derived from the same root as *tré*, meaning two, to indicate two witnesses were called to testify before a court on a previous occasion.[1] In this passage, then, *warning* means a *previous conviction*. As a consequence of these rules it was apparently decreed, in the days of the Temple, that harsher sentences should be given after a previous conviction : "If a person was punished by whipping and repeats his offence, the court puts him into prison" (M Sanhedrin IX 5). In the parallel tradition it is said : "They *warn* him once and twice, and at the third occasion they put him into prison" (T Sanhedrin XII 7). Again, *warning* connotes *previous conviction*, and serves to make the punishment harder.

Similarly, in the case of enticement to idolatry, the Sages wanted to have some kind of warning so as to be harsh with the offender,

---

[1] The equation *attested=cautioned* appears in passages such as M Baba Kama II 6: "A man is always (considered) *attested* and in M Baba Kama I 4 regarding other attested dangers. Similarly it is held in M Makkoth II 3 that "an enemy is to be put to death, because it is as if he were *attested*", and in the parallel version in T Makkoth II 10 the passage reads "an enemy shall be put to death immediately, and this is his *cautioning*".

and in this case the warning takes the form known to the later law :
"Witnesses are hidden behind the fence, and he says to him, Say what
you said to me in private; and he tells him; and he says, How can we
leave our God in Heaven and go and worship trees and stones ? If he
retracts, so much the better, but if he says, This is our duty and this
is what we should do—the people standing behind the fence bring
him to court and he is stoned" (M Sanhedrin VII 10). In this case the
warning consists of a provocative question, in order to secure evidence
of *wilfullness*.

When capital cases were no more tried, the requirement of *warning*
was interpreted as an expression of the quality of mercy. Thus it was
held : "Others liable to capital punishment may not be so sentenced
except on the strength of witnesses and *warning* and except if they
told him that he rendered himself liable to capital punishment at the
hands of a court" (T Sanhedrin XI 1).[1] The same rule was later extended
to apply to cases where the punishment was whipping ; thus it was
held : "A Nazirite who continued drinking wine all day—is liable for
one offence only. If he was told, Do not drink, do not drink—and yet he
drank—he is liable for each and every instance" (M Nazir VI 4), or
in the parallel version "in case there was only one *warning* he is liable
for one offence only; but if they *warned* him and he ate, and they
warned him and he drank—he is liable for each and every instance"
(T Neziruth IV 1).[2]

But the main function of the witness is to testify in court, and
he serves as an instrument of proof even where other means of proof
may be available.[3] Therefore the Pharisees prefer [4] the testimony of
witnesses to the real evidence indicated in the passage concerning the

---

[1] At this stage the question "did you *caution* him ?" was already included among
the seven examinations applicable to capital cases (M Sanhedrin V 1). And cf. M Makkoth
I 9.

[2] In the time of R. Judah the Prince, *cautioning* was even required in civil cases where
the result would be to deny a woman her rights under a marriage contract (T Kethuboth V 7, VII 7), and at that time it could be held : "If one of them was found to be
a relative or *unqualified*—their testimony is void .... Rabbi (Judah the Prince) says,
there is no difference in this regard between civil and capital cases. (This rule applies)
if they were *cautioned*; but if they were not *cautioned*—what should two brothers do
if they see someone killing another ?" (M Makkoth I 8).

[3] Cf. TJ Sanhedrin VI 3.23b; Sanhedrin 43b; Falk, HL 66.

[4] See Scholium to Megillath Ta'anith; Lichtenstein, HUCA VIII-IX (1931-2) 331;
Finkelstein, Pharisees, II 739 f. On the other hand, the expression was given a literal
construction by R. Eliezer (in TB—R. Eliezer b. Jacob), who also interpreted "an eye for
an eye" literally.

slanderer of a virgin : (Deut. XXII 13) : 'I found not in thy daughter
the tokens of virginity'—here are *witnesses* that she played the harlot
in her father's house; 'and yet these are the tokens of my daughter's
virginity'—here are *witnesses* to contradict his witnesses; 'and they
shall spread the garment before the elders of the city'— the facts
will be as clear as a garment. And this is one of the passages where
R. Ishmael used to expound the Torah as an allegory (Sifre, Ki Teṣe
235-237). This is a rational form of evidence and it was considered
better than arguments as to virginity and production of the garment
as evidence.[1]

There is a duty to testify in court regarding a matter being tried :
"And in case you ask, why do we need this trouble ?—It has already
been said, 'he being a witness, whether he hath seen or known, if he
do not utter it, then he shall bear his iniquity' " (Lev. V 1 ; M Sanhedrin
IV 5).[2] A party who wishes to call a witness may compel him to testify
by having an oath administered to him : "The oath of testimony
applies to men and not to women, to strangers and not to relatives,
to the qualified and not to the disqualified; it does not apply except
in regard to people eligible as witnesses, whether before the court or
not" (M Shebu'othIV 1). A party in need of testimony could "stand in
the synagogue and say, 'I adjure you that if you know anything that
can serve as testimony in my behalf—you shall come and testify for
me' " (M Shebu'oth IV 11), even if no particular person was intended.[3]
The court itself, however, would not summon witnesses to appear
before it.[4]

The passage in the Mishna dealing with the oath of testimony
specifies which people were not qualified to testify at that time, and
who thus were not compellable. These were women, relatives and other
disqualified persons (for their definition see *infra*); foreigners and
slaves were not mentioned at this stage. On the other hand other
classes are mentioned in M Baba Kama I 3 : "And by witnesses who

---

[1] Cf. also the interpretation of Ex. XXII 12 : "let him bring it for witness—let him
bring witnesses" (Mekhilta *ibid.*, TB Baba Kama 10b).

[2] Philo, Laws II 26, interprets this passage as obliging anyone who knows that an
offence of false swearing has been commited to come forward and testify in court against
the offender; see Belkin, Philo 151 ff.; and so also in the Damascus Covenant IX 17;
Rabin, QS, 110.

[3] Cf. A. Aptowitzer, Bitzaron (Hebrew) II 1940 75; Cohen, JRL 734 ff.

[4] As was the case in Hellenistic law in Egypt : W. Hellebrand, Prozesszeugniss, 61 ff.,
88 ff.

are *freemen and Jewish*"; in this passage we need not assume that the list of classes is exhaustive. [1]

Foreigners were undoubtedly not eligible to testify, but with regard to slaves the halakha perhaps only gradually became more stringent. Ecclesiasticus XXIII 10 is acquainted with testimony of a slave being taken under beating : "as a servant who is constantly being questioned lacketh not the marks of a blow".[2] Slaves may first have been disqualified in matters of torts only, since their injury is bad and they cannot be testified against in tort.[3] Josephus Antiquities IV 8.15.219, refers to women and slaves as being unqualified to testify. At a later date, the Sages of Yabne believed women in certain cases "where the testimony was such as women are qualified for" (T Kethuboth I 6).[4]

Deaf-mutes, lunatics and minors were also not considered qualified to testify, because they could not be testified against. As to a minor, his testimony was inacceptable even if only at the time of the act he had been a minor and by the time he appeared in court to testify he had attained his majority : "Said R. Eleazar b. Ṣadok : I was an infant astride my father's shoulder, and I saw a priest's daughter who had played the harlot and she was surrounded by bundles of twigs and was burnt. They said to him : You were an infant, and *an infant cannot testify*" (T Sanhedrin IX 11).[5]

The classes of persons unqualified to testify were specified only at the end of the Temple period, when the aloofness of the Pharisees, the *associates* and the *trusted persons* from the common people became marked. Disqualification may have taken the place of the doctrine according to which the priestly circles held themselves apart : "In previous times, marriage contracts were signed either by priests or by Levites or by other Israelites who intermarry with the priesthood"

---

[1] See however Cohen, JRL, 128 f.

[2] As to the testimony—and torture—of slaves in Greek and Roman law : Hellebrand, *op. cit.* 95 ff. In M Sanhedrin III 3 slaves were not counted among the *unqualified* to testify, but they were included in the list in M Rosh Hashanah I 8. As to the torture of a slave-woman to examine her testimony see Josephus, Antiquities XVII 4.1.64; I War XXX 2-3, 584-586.

[3] See *supra*, p. 40.

[4] Cf. M Rosh Hashanah I 8.

[5] See M Kethuboth II 1, and Lieberman, Tos. Kif. Megillah II 8. A special age requirement for testimony is prescribed in the Damascus Covenant X 1 and in the Manual of Discipline I 11.

(T Sanhedrin VII 1).[1] In the course of the dispute between the Pharisees and Sadducees, the former laid down other criteria of qualification for witnesses.

The elite groups originally disqualified outsiders from being dependable witnesses; thus the Damascus Covenant X 2 : "Let no man be declared a reliable witness against his neighbour who has transgressed anything of the commandment high-handedly until he is purified so as to return". It may be assumed that the people who were *dependable* in matters of tithes denied such *dependability* from the unlearned people, and not only in matters of tithes but in other matters as well. [2] In this way a list of categories of unqualified persons was made up—and began to grow.[3]

Originally it was held : "And these are *unqualified* :the dice player, the lender on interest, people who set doves flying ... and gatherers of the harvest of the seventh year" (M Sanhedrin III 3). In a parallel Mishna, more comprehensive and apparently of a later date, dealers in the harvest of the seventh year, and slaves, were also included (M Rosh Hashanah I 8). Still later "there were added thieves, shepherds and extortioners, and everyone who is suspect in matters of property— his testimony is *inadmissible*"(T Sanhedrin V 5), and "to these there were further added shepherds, collectors and publicans" (TB Sanhedrin 25b).

With the passage of time not only people who were suspect in property matters were considered *unqualified*, but also "anybody suspected of taking pay to sit in judgment, or of taking pay to testify— every case that he tried and every testimony that he gave are void" (T Bekhoroth III 8). Thus it was also held : "A person who is suspect in a class of matters should neither try cases or give evidence in a case where that class is touched upon" (T Demai V 2).[4]

Although the *trusted persons* were depended upon in matter of tithes both as regards themselves and as regards others (M Demai

---

[1] As to witnesses whose testimony was suspect in Hellenistic Egypt see Préaux, Recueils de Société Jean Bodin XVI (1965), 212.

[2] TB Pesaḥim 49b : "Six things were said concerning *unlearned persons* : they may not be made witnesses to anything, and their testimony may not be accepted ..."

[3] See however Rabin, QS, 64 f., according to whom there were originally more disqualifications and later on the number grew smaller. As to disqualification for testifying see L. Löw, Gesammelte Schriften III, Szegedin 1873.

[4] The composition of the *disqualification* is reflected also in the order in which they are given in M Bekhoroth IV 4-10. First come those who are no expert, then those who take pay, and finally those who are suspect.

II 2), in other matters the rule was that "a person is *not dependable regarding himself*" (M Kethuboth II 9). There is a difference here between members of an elite group who rely upon one another, and the rest of the people, to whom the presumption does not apply. From this point it was a short step to disqualify relatives who were specified in the "Early Mishna : his uncle, and his cousin, and anyone eligible to be an heir of his" (M Sanhedrin III 4). To these there were later added "the close friend and the enemy" (M Sanhedrin III 5.)

Examination of the witnesses [1] was entrusted to the judges and not to the parties. Ecclesiasticus XI 8 warns the judges not to jump to conclusions as to anything being distorted and not rebuke a party until the examination of the witnesses is over : "Before thou hast examined blame not; investigate first, and afterwards rebuke". A detailed account of the examination of witnesses is furnished in the story of Susanna in the Septuagint version of Daniel 32-45.[2] Daniel demands that the witnesses be kept apart and that they be examined separately. The examination is conducted in the presence of the public; it is not said whether Susanna was herself present, but probably she was.[3] Before the decisive questions, Daniel warns the witness and reminds him of the penalty for perjury, and then he goes on to examine him :"Under which tree and in what place did you see them together ?" The examination reveals that the witnesses contradict each other, and therefore the testimony is void. In this description the fact stands out that the witnesses take no oath to tell the truth but only hear the exhortation of the judge,[4] further, no record was taken of what they said.[5]

Simon b. Shetaḥ laid great stress on the examination of the witnesses : "Be very searching in the *examination of witnesses*, and be heedful of thy words, lest through them they learn to falsify" (Aboth I 9). Judah b. Tabbai, on the other hand, wanted the parties to be examined : "Act not the counsel's part; when the parties to a suit are standing before thee, let them *both be regarded by thee as wicked;* but when they are departed from thy presence, regard them both as innocent, the verdict having been acquiesced in by them" (Aboth I 8).

---

[1] As to examination of witnesses in Hellenistic law see Hellebrand, *op. cit.* 140 f., 168 f.

[2] Regarding this story see J.D.M. Derrett, NTSt X (1963), 24 f.

[3] Regarding the presence of the parties see Hellebrand, 136, 169.

[4] On the other hand Hellebrand, 148, 169.

[5] On the other hand Hellebrand, 138.

Although witnesses were subject to examination and inquiry, and were admonished by the judge, there is no record that physical pressure was ever applied to witnesses who were freemen. Only Herod applied torture to a number of women in his court, some slave and some free, when he was investigating an accusation of poisoning.[1] There was also no reason to apply pressure to an accused person, for at least in the view of later halakha "a man cannot *incriminate himself*", and thus his confession could have no bearing on the outcome of the trial.

The order of examination of witnesses according to the Mishna, which has been preserved in three versions for civil cases, for capital cases and for sanctification of the new month,[2] resembles the descriptions given above. The examination proper is conducted *in camera* : "everybody was sent out" (M Sanhedrin III 6), so that no one might wisper to the witnesses what to say. In this context it is remarkable that the services of the judges' scribes were not utilised to record what the witnesses said and thus facilitate the examination as to whether or not they corroborated each other.[3]

From the admonishment of the witnesses prior to their testimony in capital cases we can gather what the substance of the testimony was and what testimony was inadmissible : "Perchance ye will say what is but *supposition* or *hearsay*, or at *secondhand* or 'we *heard it* from a dependable person' ?" (M Sanhedrin IV 5). The witnesses must testify from personal knowledge, and from no other source.[4] Another rule, which was certainly current during the days of the Temple was that " 'we have not seen' affords no proof" (M Eduyoth II 2).

False witnesses were punished according to the provisions of Deut. XIX 16-21.[5] In the story of Susanna mentioned above, the falseness of the testimony became evident immediately after the trial ended, and the trial of the witnesses was, appended to that of the accused woman. The purpose of the proceeding was not to punish the witnesses but rather acquit the accused woman, but as a result of this acquittal— and of the law of the Torah—the witnesses are both to be put to

---

[1] Josephus, Antiquities XVII 4.1.64; I War XXX 2-3, 584-586.

[2] M Sanhedrin III 6, IV 5-V 4; M Rosh Hasanah II 6.

[3] The scribes would note only the words of the judges : M Sanhedrin IV 3, V 5.

[4] As to conclusions reached by witnesses in Hellenistic law and other rules of that system see Hellebrand, 170 ff.

[5] Regarding the law concerning false witnesses see, *inter alia :* B. Revel, JQR III, (1912-13) 344 f.; J. Horowitz, Festschrift D. Hoffmann, Berlin 1914, 139 ff.; Finkelstein. Pharisees 696 ff., 843, 899; A. Arazi, Torah shebeal Pe (Hebrew), IV (1962) 114-121; P. Daykan, Sinai (Hebrew), LVI (1965) 295-302.

death. [1] They are treated as false witnesses due to the fact that they contradicted each other regarding the place of the alleged act. Such a contradiction is taken as proof that they bore false testimony— and it justifies the application of the law regarding *scheming witnesses*.

These rules of halakha were of importance in the dispute between the Pharisees and the Sadducees. The former held, as in the story of Susanna : "False witnesses are not to be put to death unless the trial is over; for the Sadducees say : unless the accused person has been put to death" (M Makkoth I 6).[2] Indeed, the Pharisees would impose a sentence of death only if another set of witnesses came forward and revealed the *scheme* in the testimony of the first set by testifying that they were with them somewhere else at the time of the act : "How can you testify—for you were with us on that day at place X—these are *scheming* witnesses, and they may be put to death on the strength of such an accusation" (Makkoth I 4). However, mere contradictions between the testimonies of sets of witnesses, or between the original witnesses themselves, do not involve the rigour of the law against *scheming* witnesses, but only leads to all the testimony being cancelled out (M Makkoth *ibid.*, Sanhedrin V 2).[3]

Although the biblical passage speaks of a false witness, it was held by the Pharisees in the days of Simon b. Shetaḥ, that no death penalty could be imposed unless both witnesses were shown to have been *scheming* (TB Makkoth 5b, TJ Sanhedrin VI 5, 23b). Until that time it was perhaps possible to apply the rigour of the law even to one of the witnesses only, just as it could be applied in the case of two witnesses contradicting each other. Judah b. Tabbai originally adhered to the old doctrine, but later on he accepted the position taken by Simon b. Shetaḥ.

5. PARTY'S ADMISSION

Before dealing with the subject of oaths as a means of clarifying the truth in court, it may already be stressed at this point that an oath imposed on a defendant is intended to induce him to admit the sub-

---

[1] As to the law regarding false witnesses in Hellenistic Egypt and its main purpose to rescind the original judgment : Hellebrand, 188, ff.; Préaux, Recueil Société Jean Bodin XVI (1965) 218 ff.

[2] See *supra*, p. 39.

[3] Later on there developed a difference of opinion between the Houses of Hillel and Shammai regarding the details of the law on contradictory witnesses : TB Baba Bathra 41 b.

stance of the action against him. If a party admits in court that his opponent's position is correct, there is no need to continue the trial any longer, since "a party's admission is equivalent to a hundred witnesses" (T Baba Meṣia I 10). At the end of the Second Commonwealth the rules of admission were extended to include constructive admission : "If a man contest another's ownership of a field, but has himself signed (the deed of sale) as a witness ... he has himself signed (the deed of sale) as a witness ... he has lost his title. If he made (the field) a boundary mark for (the field of) another, he has lost his title" (M Kethuboth XIII 6).

Moreover, even an admission out of court is binding on the party (M Sanhedrin III 6) and the very use of bills is no more than the use of an admission out of court which can later on be proved in court.

Further, in matters of *prohibition and permission*,[1] especially in matrimonial affairs, the judges are to rely on the oral admission of a concerned person if it is to his detriment. A person is dependable when he implicitly *prohibits* himself in regard to something; thus a woman may admit that she is married, or that she is impure, and her admission is taken as proof against her.[2]

The ancient halakha during the Second Commonwealth may have been familiar with the examination of the accused in court, and if he was a slave—he may have been examined under torture.[3] The passage in Deut. XVII 6, "at the mouth of two witnesses, or three witnesses, shall he that is to die be put to death" may have been interpreted as applying only where the accused remained silent, and not where he confessed. Just as we assumed that the Sages instituted the laws concerning *cautioning*, in relief of the rigour of the law, when capital cases were no longer tried, the same tendency towards leniency may be noted in the denial validity of an accused person's confession. It may be assumed that in case of incitement to idolatry the accused could be convicted on the strength of his confession, even if there were no witnesses and *cautioning* : "all persons liable to the penalty of death according to the Torah may not be put to death *according to them* except an inciter to idolatry" (T Sanhedrin X 11)—a passage which should be construed to mean that they may not be put to death

---

[1] See p. 16. note 3.

[2] In the words of the Sages of the Talmud : she has *declared herself forbidden*.

[3] As to the law in biblical times see Falk, HL, 70. As to examination and confession of the accused in Roman law see : G. Broggini, Coniectanea, 152 f., 172; Recueils Société Jean Bodin XVI (1965) 242 f., 262; G. Pugliese, *ibid*. 331.

on the strength of *their own words*, except an inciter, who may be put
to death on the strength of *his own words*, that is to say, upon his
confession. "Another person liable to the penalty of death may not
be convicted except on the strength of testimony of witnesses and
cautioning which expressly conveyed to him that he would be liable
to the death penalty in court" (T *ibid.* XI 1). The requirement of
witnesses and *caution*, in other words : the rule not to rely on the
accused person's confession, was applied as a matter of leniency in
other capital cases.

In M Sanhedrin VI 2, the confession of the accused is transferred
to the place of stoning : "they say to him, *confess*, for it is usual for
those who are to be put to death to confess, for anyone who confesses
has a portion in the world to come". This is a new meaning of the
accused person's confession, a meaning given to it after it was dis-
allowed as evidence.[1]

6. Oath

Although Scripture provides only for a *bailee's oath* (Ex. XXII
6-14), it was apparently allowed, for any plaintiff who brought no
evidence, to demand that the defendant take an oath in denial of the
claim. But since the law of oaths was first enunciated in connection
with bail, the Mishna (Shebu'oth V 1-5) included under the term
oath of bail all oaths taken in order to avoid payment. Such oaths were
part of the practice of the Jews of Elephantine; the Aramaic bills
mention actions for land and for chattels, actions for damages and a
suit of a divorced woman, in all of which an oath was imposed on the
defendant to be absolved from claims of the plaintiff.[2]

An oath was certainly imposed in cases of fiduciary relationship
between plaintiff and defendant. Among the Jews of Elephantine

---

[1] Later on it was held that a person who confesses to an act for which he must pay
a sum other than mere damages is exempt from payment (M Kethuboth III 9, Shebu'oth
V 4). Yet Raba finds it difficult to show the reason in the rule that "a person cannot
constitute himself wicked", and he falls back on the assumption that "a person is *near*
to himself", and as Rashi comments "the Torah *disqualified relatives* from testifying"
(TB Sanhedrin 9b).

[2] See Cowley, AP No. 6, 7, 14, 44, 45; Yaron, Introduction, 32 f. As to the exonerative
oath of the defendant in Hellenistic law, see E. Seidl, Der Eid im ptolemäischen Recht,
München 1929, 64, 98; E. Seidl, Der Eid im römisch-ägyptischen Provinzialrecht, I,
(MB 17), München 1933, 106, 108; II (*dto.*, 24), 1935, 94 f. Regarding oaths in the halakha
see also E.E. Halevi, Tarbiz (Hebrew) XXXVII (1968) 24-29.

the husband could impose an oath on his divorced wife before returning her property to her, and the wife must take the oath even though there be no specific allegation against her.[1] Similarly the Sages held that a woman is not to be paid under her marriage contract unless she takes an oath (M Gittin IV 3), but later the onus of swearing was restricted to special cases (M Shebu'oth VII 7, following M Kethuboth IX 7). Such an oath is basically an oath of a defendant against whom nothing definite is alleged; thus a wife is suspected of having retained property of her husband, and only after she has cleared herself of the suspicion is she allowed to take what is due to her.[2]

Similarly, an oath may be imposed on these, although no allegation is proferred against them : jointholders, tenants, trustees, a wife that manages the affairs of the house, and the managing co-heir" (M Shebu'oth VII 8). All these hold property in trust, and have to clear themselves by oath of all suspicion of having retained anything. At the same time there was a marked tendency to refrain from administering oaths. This tendency was a result of an increase in false oaths, which indicated the limited value of this mode for reaching the truth. Ecclesiasticus XXIII 9-11 exhorts the reader not to take a habit of the naming of the Holy One, "for as a servant who is constantly being questioned lacketh not the marks of a blow, so also he that sweareth and is continually naming the name of the Lord is not free from sins. A man of many oaths is filled with iniquity, and the scourge departeth not from his house; if he offend his sin will be upon him and if he disregard it he sinneth doubly; and if he sweareth without need he shall not be justified, for his house shall be filled with calamities".[3]

It became difficult to be sure of the truth of an oath without a sanction imposed by man in case the lie became evident. It is possible that the culprit was in certain cases punished by whipping,[4] but in most such cases only divine punishment was invoked, and the perjurer

---

[1] Cowley, AP 14; Yaron, Introduction, 63.

[2] It is this oath that is referred to in M Kethuboth IX 1.

[3] The Essenes especially objected to oaths : Josephus, II War VIII 6. 134. But the Pharisees also apparently relied on the prohibition of taking oaths in vain when they refused to swear allegiance to Herod : Josephus, Antiquities XVII 2. 4. 42. Other expressions against oaths are to be found in Philo, Laws II 2-5, the Ten Commandments 84-86; Testaments of the Twelve Patriarchs, Gad VI 4; and see I. Heinemann, Judaica, Festschritt H. Cohen, Berlin 1912, 109 ff.; Lieberman, Hellenism 214 ff.; and Albeck, Mishna, Shebu'oth, Introduction.

[4] Philo, Laws II 27-28; Belkin, Philo 148 f.,; Seidl, Eid im römisch-ägyptischen Provinzialrecht I 122.

was required to bring a sacrifice if he confessed (M Shebu'oth V 1, VIII 3).[1]

The courts thus came to restrict the case of oaths. The *bailee's oath* prescribed in the Torah was imposed only in actions of bail but not in actions such as "you have violated, or seduced, my daughter",[2] "you have stolen my ox", "your ox has killed my ox", "you have wounded me or bruised me" (M Shebu'oth V 4). Even the *bailee's oath* was imposed only if the bailee denied the bail in part, whereas if he denied it totally—the decisive oath no longer applied.[3]

Similarly, the onus of swearing which lay on a woman claiming under her marriage contract was restricted to cases where less than the full sum was claimed, or where a single witness testified that the sum had already been paid, or the like (M Kethuboth IX 7).[4]

At the end of the Second Commonwealth there apparently began a reverse process, towards increased use of the decisive oath. A defendant admitting part of a claim, even when the action was not one of bail, would be obliged to take an oath,[5] and it was therefore ordained that "a person who found a lost article need not swear, as a *precaution for the general good*" (M Gittin V 3). A whole series of oaths was introduced by the *judges of decrees* in Jerusalem (M Kethuboth XIII 1-4), and other rules of halakha requiring an oath may also be ascribed to this period.[6]

Following the rule disqualifying certain classes of persons from giving testimony (M Sanhedrin III 3),[7] the same classes were declared *suspect regarding oaths* (M Shebu'oth VII 4). But in order that the sinner should have no gain, and in view of the fact that in the meantime the case of oaths increased, it was held that "these take an oath in order to recover under their own action : a person hired, robbed or

---

[1] And even the obligation to bring a sacrifice was greatly restricted-e.g. in connection with the oath of testimony : M Shebu'oth IV 3-13, in connection with the oath of bail, *ibid.* V 4-5.

[2] A similar case : Seidl, Eid im römisch-ägyptischen Provinzialrecht I 108.

[3] See Albeck, Mishna, Shebu'oth, Introduction, 240.

[4] Similarly, a partial admission of a claim to land was held not to involve an oath (M Shebu'oth VI 3, 5).

[5] Cf. de Vries, Tarbiz (Hebrew) XXXVI (1967) 229 ff.

[6] Eg. the oath of the two who hold a garment and claim it (M Baba Meṣia I 1), the oath to contradict a single witness (Sifre on Deut. XIX 15 : One witness shall not use up against a man) which is an extension of M Kethuboth IX 7, and the oath of the heirs (M Shebu'oth VII 7) as indicated.

[7] See *supra* p. 123.

wounded, a person whose adversary is *suspect regarding oaths*, and a shopkeeper in support of his account-books" (M Shebu'oth VII 1).

7. POSSESSION AND PRESUMPTION [1]

The structure of the family at the beginning of the Second Common- wealth, and the laws of the Jubilee then practiced, tended to weaken the position of private ownership of land and instead to strengthen that of *possession*. At that time land was acquired by *possession* both in the case of family land handed over to the possession of a member of the family and in the case of land that previously was *res nullius* (M Qiddushin I 5, Baba Bathra III 3). Once a person became so posses- sed of land, it could no longer be taken away from him, even though *possession*, as a mode of acquisition was perhaps inferior to purchase by money or by deed.[2] At a later time the rules of *possession* were extended to apply to slaves, since they were transferred together with the land and therefore a Canaanite slave could also be acquired by *possession* (M Qiddushin I 3).

Regarding chattels it seems that originally only ownership was protected by law, and not mere possession. An animal could indeed be acquired by delivery, by lifting or by drawing (M Qiddushin I 4), but such acquisition was not based on *continued* possession but on the *act* of taking possession. But at the end of the Second Common- wealth the halakha protected *possession* of chattels also, especially in cases where ownership was uncertain. Thus the House of Hillel held that "if a woman awaiting levirate marriage ... dies ... her property remains with the *possessors*" (M Yebamoth IV 3). In this case a doubt arose as to who are the woman's heirs both in regard to land and in regard to chattels, and the solution is to abide by *possession*.[3]

---

[1] In this section we examine the semantic development of the Hebrew term *ḥazaqa*, meaning possession, occupation as well as presumption.

[2] The term *possession* was synonymous with *acquisition* :"As soon as he took *possession* of one of them he *acquired* (the Erfurt MS T Kethuboth II 1, TJ Qiddushin I 5, 60c reads : *possessed*) all of them". As to possession as a mode of acquisition in Roman law see Kaser, RPR, I, 358 f.

[3] See also the dictum of R. Judah in T Baba Meṣia VIII 23 : "The young is always in the possession of the seller". In the opinion of R. Yosé in T Aboda Zara III (IV) 11, possession of slaves is important in resolving doubts not only regarding ownership but also regarding the status itself. *Possession* is thus decisive in the matter of a slave being Jewish or Gentile : "Slaves *possessed* by a Jew, even though they are uncircumcised, are to be regarded as Canaanites, until they give notice that they are children of slave-

Possession was originally taken in the presence of witnesses and of all the parties affected, and therefore the element of time was not decisive ;[1] but in case anyone claims title to the land and argues that he had no notice of the taking of *possession*, a period of time had to pass without any adverse claim being raised. At the end of the Second Commonwealth it was apparently held that three years of *possession* had to pass in case of land (M Baba Bathra III 1).[2] This period applied only in cases where the possessor and the claimant lived in the same country (M Baba Bathra III 2).[3] Further, possession was limited as a mode of acquisition to such cases only where it was accompanied by an *allegation of title* (M Baba Bathra III 3) ; yet a possessor by virtue of inheritance need not make such an *allegation* (*ibid.*) [4] and later it was held that a possessor by virtue of purchase need not make such an *allegation* (M Baba Bathra II 5, III 8). In order to preclude deceit certain classes of possessors were denied acquisition, in cases of fiduciary relationship between them and the claimant (M Baba Bathra III 3).

All these rules of halakha restricted the application of acquisition by *possession* where the original act was not performed in the presence, and with the consent, of all the affected parties. With the strengthening of the institution of private ownership, *possession* as a mode of acquisition became restricted. Finally it was held that even a person acquiring by *possession* must pay money (T Kethuboth II 1). [5]

Possessory presumptions were also to be found in matters of *usufruct* and even in spiritual matters such as the priestly shares between each other and between them and the rest of the people. In the days of Neḥemiah substantive genealogical proof was still insisted upon : "These sought their register, that is, the genealogy, but it was not found ; therefore were they deemed *polluted* and put from the priest-

---

women who were not immersed. Slaves *possesed* by Cuthites (=Samaritans), if they are circumcised, are to be regarded as Cuthites, until they give notice that they are the children of Canaananite slave-women. Slaves *possessed* by Gentiles, even if they are circumcised, are to be regarded as Gentiles". As to possession in Roman law see Kaser, RPR, I, 122 ff,. 316 ff.; and as to possession in the halakha : Z. Warhaftig, Possession in Jewish Law (Hebrew), Jerusalem 1964.

[1] Such taking of possession is described in the purchase of the Cave of Machpelah and in the redemption by Boaz, and is the act referred to in M Qiddushin I 3, 5.

[2] With regard to such a provision in Roman law see Kaser, RPR, I 353 ff.

[3] Cf. Kaser, RPR I, 358.

[4] Cf. Kaser, RPR I, 354.

[5] And see Lieberman, Tos. Kif. *ad loc.*

hood : And the *Tirshatha* said unto them, that they should not eat of
the most holy things, till there stood up a priest with *Urim* and with
Thummim" (Ezra II 62-63). [1] But as time passed it became possible to
rely on possessory presumption instead of a genealogical document.
"R. Yose says *Possession* (Presumption by prescription) is a great
thing ... you remain in your *possession*, that just as you ate of the
Holy Things of the countryside in the diaspora you may do likewise
here" (TB Kethuboth 24b). [2]

Although it was held that a priest marrying a woman should trace
her descent to be sure that she is eligible to marry a priest, there are a
number of *possessory presumptions* that may be relied upon : "Descent
need not be traced beyond the altar (where her father ministered as a
priest) or beyond the platform (where her father sang as a Levite)
or beyond the Sanhedrin (of which her father was a member), and of
all whose fathers are known to have been public officers or almoners
may marry priests, and (the prospective husband) need not trace
their descent" (M Qiddushin IV 5).

Possessory presumptions also served as a basis for the arrangement
of *wards* of priests and Levites in the Temple service. Although an
unlearned person wishing to join the class of the *Trusted* must give
an undertaking (M Demai II 2), he may yet have in his favour a *presumption that he is trusted for tithes*" (T Demai III 6-8). This *presumption*
is not based, however, on the use of a right by a person claiming title
to it ; [3] it is more similar to a *presumption* of fact, to which we now may
turn.

Such a *presumption* is apparently conceived originally in concrete
fashion. The person or thing to which the presumption applies is
considered to be *possessed* by a group of people, i.e. he is presumed to
be a member of the group comprising every body to which the pre-

---

[1] According to Apocryphal Ezra V 40 they were deprived of certain holy things,
meaning lesser holy things and heave-offerings.

[2] Cf. T Pe'ah IV 5, Kethuboth III 3 (But they are not reliable for the *possession* of
priestly office").

[3] Cf. M Ḥagiga II 6, where *possession* is based on actual use of a right. The same
element appears in the case of the term to denote a *lenient custom*, where the community
is treated as though it has acquired the right to act in accordance with its custom :
"And they became *possessed of the right* to allow a woman to marry on the grounds
of hearsay evidence or on the evidence of a slave, a woman, or a slave-woman" (M
Yebamoth XVI 7).

sumption may properly apply.[1] A judge may not decide according to his own discretion, but only according to the rules of evidence. These rigid rules do not furnish an answer to all the questions, and there was therefore a need for presumptions of fact to govern the onus of proof and even substantive rights.

A few examples as to how presumptions of fact are created by classification and generalisation : "... because a proselyte woman was presumed chaste and a freed bondwoman presumed unchaste" (T Horayoth II 11). Women in general are here classified in two groups, chaste and unchaste, and thus every woman appearing in court is *possessed* by one of these groups.[2] In like manner every defendant can be assigned to one of two groups i.e. those who are liable and those who are not, and the onus of proof will be accordingly : "If the wall of a courtyard fell down ... each jointholder may be *presumed* to have paid (his share in restoring it) unless (another jointholder) brings evidence that he did not" (M Baba Bathra I 4).[3] Oxen are also divided into harmless and attested, and once an ox has been attested to *it remains in that presumption* (M Baba Kama IV 4).[4]

8. Bills

At the beginning of the Second Commonwealth there already existed set forms of bills for various purposes.[5] In public law special importance attached to *bills of genealogy*, since the returning exiles traced their descent according to their families and tribes (Neh. XI, I Chronicles IX). According to such genealogical documents distinctions were drawn between "ten castes of which some were eligible for intermarriage and some were not (M Qiddushin IV 1). The priests themselves

---

[1] *Possession* in the concrete meaning appears at places like M Terumoth X 8.

[2] Cf. M Kethuboth I 6, Gittin III 3.

[3] Cf. M Bekhoroth VIII 6.

[4] A person classifying an individual confronting him, in accordance with one of these rules, is "*possessed* regarding him that he is a ..." (see T Kethuboth V 1, Baba Bathra VII 3, Ohaloth XVII 5). In this case the subjective aspect is stressed; as distinct from the usual presumption of fact which is laid down by law. As to presumption in Roman law see: Kaser, RZPR 279, 487, who remarks that it first appeared after the Classic period, and thus after the days of the Sages of the Mishna.

[5] Regarding written testimony see : J. Ph. Lévy, American University Law Review XIII (1964) 133-153. As to the documents in Jeremiah XXXII, and in the Talmud compared with Gen. XXIII and Ruth IV : E. Volterra, Synteleia V. Arangio-Ruiz (Biblioteca di Labeo), Napoli 1966, 1190-97.

were registered in a genealogical book in the Temple, "and there they would sit and trace the descent of priests and Levites" (T Sanhedrin VII 1).

It is possible that the Hasmonean kings kept lists of arms bearing men according to the families, on the basis of which the halakha ruled that anyone appearing in such lists may be deemed eligible : "They need not trace descent ... any whose name was recorded in the king's army" (M Qiddushin IV 5). Remnants of *genealogical scrolls* were apparently stored away, and may have been discovered after the Destruction (TJ Ta'anith IV 2, 68a; TB Pesaḥim 62b).[1]

Although no private bills from the period of the Return have as yet come to light, it may be assumed that they resembled the Aramaic bills of Elephantine in Egypt.[2] There has recently been discovered a series of bills of Samaria written at the end of the Persian period, and it is likely to clarify to what extent the custom in Palestine corresponded to the forms of writing of the Jews of Egypt.[3] Further, there are existent many Greek bills from Egypt written by Jews, and these bills may serve as a clue to the understanding of Greek influence on Jewish practice.[4] Of major importance for our better knowledge of pre-Destruction halakha are the bills that have been discovered in the Dead Sea region since 1950. These bills, originating in the generations just before and after the Destruction and written in Hebrew, Aramaic and Greek, demonstrate the precision of Talmudic halakha handed down to us in sources of later date.[5]

As to the form of bills in use in Palestine during the Second Commonwealth, it seems that the *tied bill* gave way, in the course of time,

---

[1] Regarding a census in Ptolemaic kingdom and its application to the Jews see III Maccabees II 28-30, IV 14, VI 38; and as to registration of the population in the Hellenistic world : Ch Préaux, Recueil Société J. Bodin XVI (1965) 162 ff.

[2] The Elephantine documents were printed in Cowley, AP; Kraeling, AP; and see Yaron, Introduction, see also JJS XII (1961) 165 ff. Regarding divorce in Elephantine see : E. Volterra, Studi Orientalistici G. Levi Della Vida. Roma 1956, II, 586-600.

[3] F.M. Cross, BA XXVI (1963) 110 ff.

[4] These bills were printed and commented upon in CPJ. In connection with the Greek influence in matters of divorce see J. Modrzejewski, Iura XII (1961) 162-193, and also E. Volterra, JJP XV (1965), 21-28.

[5] To date there have appeared DJD II, and a description of the bills found by Israeli scholars in Israel Exploration Society Journal XXVI (1962) 139-243. See also the review by R. Yaron, JJS XI (1960) 157-171; E. Volterra, Iura (1963) 29-70. A summary of all the material published is given by E. Koffmann, Die Doppelurkunden aus der Wüste Juda (Studies on the Texts of the Desert of Juda), Leiden 1968; cf. Biblica L (1969) 414 ff.; TRG XXXVII (1969) 261 ff.

to the *simple bill*. Writing the full text on both sides of the bill was no longer required, and it was considered sufficient to indicate the contents of the bill on the reverse side; on the other hand, the witnesses signed the bill proper, instead of impressing their seals on the outside seal. This, anyhow, was the accepted procedure in the bills of Elephantine,[1] and perhaps the idea of signing on the face of the bill was adopted also in the covenant concluded at the same time in Judea (Neh. X 1 ff.).[2] Nevertheless, the *tied bill* remained in use in the Judean desert and is mentioned in the Mishna (M Baba Bathra X 1-2). Sometimes also appear the signatures of the scribe (M Gittin IX 8) and of the party giving the undertaking.[3]

In the bills of Elephantine the terms of a bill are not repeated on the reverse side : only its salient points are indicated there in one line; in the bills of the Judean desert, however, the terms of the bill were still set out in full twice : The tied bill mentioned in the Mishna was apparently written after the fashion of the Judean desert bills, whereas the simple bill is closer to the bills of Elephantine.

The main value of a bill is evidential, and therefore the signature of the witnesses was more important than of the party giving the undertaking. *Notes of hand* without witnesses were also in use, either in form of a letter or in the form of a bill.[4] In the Book of Tobias V 3 a *note-of-hand* is mentioned as if it were a bill in proof of a loan, and according to the longer version the document is even torn in two and each of the parties is given a half. This was indeed the practice of the medieval *chirographum*, and is apparently a medieval interpolation.

In any event it was possible to create a promissory note by the promisor writing out the full text by his own hand and if the plaintiff produced the defendant's *note-of-hand* to the effect that he owes him-the debt may be recovered from unmortgaged property (M Baba Bathra X 8). At about the same time there appeared what was considered an unusual type of *note-of-hand*, which was only signed by the promisor but not written by him.R. Ḥanina, the prefect of the

---

[1] See Yaron, Introduction, and Gulak, Urkundenwesen, 25. As to tied bill see also Koffmahn, *passim* and D. Piattelli, Rivista Italiana per le Scienze Giuridiche XI Ser. III (1963-67), 381 ff.

[2] The same procedure is found in the Demotic bill in Egypt : E. Seidl, Aegyptische Rechtsgeschichte der Saiten und Perserzeit, Aegyptologische Forschungen. 20, Glückstadt, 1968, 17.

[3] Thus also in the Dead Sea bills but not in the Talmudic bill : Gulak, Urkundenwesen, 19.

[4] As to this form in Greek and Hellenistic law : Seidl, PtRG, 56, 61.

priests, testified that there was "a little village near Jerusalem, and an old man lived there, and he used to lend to all the villagers, and he would write out the note in his own hand and others would sign; and a case came before the Sages and they allowed it" (M Eduyoth II 3).[1]

Bills of divorcement were also frequently written by the husband himself, but it was usual to add the signatures of the witnesses to that of the husband, as is the case in Murabbaat 19. However, even a bill of divorcement without the signature of witnesses was declared permissible, if the bill was handed by him to her in the presence of witnesses, and perhaps even if he gave it to her when they were alone (M Gittin IX 4). In this latter case, however, there was a danger that the husband would deny his signature and cast a slur on the bill of divorcement, and it was therefore decreed that "the witnesses sign the bill of divorcement as a *precaution for the general good*" (*ibid.*, and IV 3).[2]

The purpose of every bill is to retain the testimony, so as to make it unnecessary to call witnesses and take their evidence orally.[3] It was therefore necessary to write exactly what was said or done at the time, and thus the bill would serve as minutes of the transaction. Hence the common style in the bills of Elephantine, of the Judean desert and of the Talmud, the parties or one of them using direct

---

[1] The use of the verb *allow* may indicate that the term was first used in the case of a bill of divorcement, where it is proper, and later on it was adopted for use in case of loans. Cf. Gulak, Urkundenwesen, 12 ff. A Jewish *note-of-hand* in Greek is P. Murabbaat 114.

[2] This decree led to subsequent strictness. Originally it was held that "if he wrote out (the bill of divorcement) in his own handwriting but there were no witnesses ... it is a doubtful divorce" (M Yebamoth III 8); later on a stricture was added : "Three kinds of bills of divorcement are invalid, yet if she married again the offspring is legitimate : one, that a man wrote his own hand but there were no witnesses to it ..." (M Gittin IX 4). Only R. Elazar maintains his view that the signature of the witnesses is unnecessary, and that the witnesses of delivery are decisive; he holds that a *note-of-hand* is valid enough to effect recovery from charged property, at least if it was delivered in the presence of witnesses. R. Elazar thus dissents from M Baba Bathra X 8 and Gittin II 5. In his opinion, and apparently according to the halakha from the time of the Temple, "a woman may write out her own bill of divorcement" (M Eduyoth II 3, Gittin II 5), with only the husband signing, and not the witnesses, and "if he produced against the defendant his *note-of-hand* that he owes him"—he may recover from charged property (M Gittin IX 4, contrary to Baba Bathra X 8).

[3] The bill takes the place of an act in the presence of witnesses as described, e.g., in Ruth IV 8-9.

speech;[1] when only one of the parties is quoted the witnesses might add, in indirect speech, the reaction of the other party, to the effect that he agreed to the terms just set forth. In the course of time the indirect style became accepted in formulas of bills : "Both in case there is written in it : *'A borrowed from B'* and in case there is written in it *'I A the son of B have borrowed from C'*, and the witnesses signed below—it is valid" (T Baba Bathra XI 4).[2]

A bill generally testifies to the admission of one party that the other has a right. Such an admission is needed in order to perpetuate the present condition of mutual rights and to avoid future disputes. If property is involved, one party asserts "no right and no dispute" or "I have neither right nor claim" (M Kethuboth IX 1, TB Baba Bathra 43a).[3]

An admission need not be given before a judge or any other official authority; the presence of witnesses would be sufficient.[4] In an Aramaic promissory note of the year 55/56 B.C.E., found in the cave of Murabbaat, after the date and place are indicated—the first word is "it has been *admitted*".[5] The term, however, may have been used in its context in a wider sense, that of *giving notice*, since the subsequent text appears to refer to the lender and not to the borrower. This bill, moreover, contains not only an admission but also the fact of the loan itself : "He counted and gave me silver in the sum of twenty zuz" : thus witnesses testify to the act proper and not merely to an admission of it.[6]

A bill granting title and even a bill of divorcement, was originally

---

[1] As to the origin of this form in Neo-Babylonian law see H. Petschow, Journal of Cuneiform Studies XIX (1965) 103-120.

[2] Compare TJ Qiddushin I 2, 59a : "I, A, have given my daughter in betrothal to B", and TB Gittin 85b : "that A, son of B, released and divorced B his wife, who had been his wife, from this day on forever" (Munich MS version).

[3] This formula is found in the Elephantine documents : Yaron, Introduction, 30, 81. It served mainly as a waiver clause in relation to future action, a waiver which was necessary in the absence of a doctrine of res judicata : Yaron *ibid.* 103. See also JJS XII. (1961) 168. This technique was familiar in Babylonia and Egypt : Seidl, PtRG, 5, 51, 99,

[4] However, the admission regarding a testament, deposited in the Jewish *archeia* in Alexandria in 13 B.C.E. (CPJ II, 143), was delivered in the presence of the notary according to Hellenistic legal practice.

[5] And see Koffmahn, 80 ff.; Mur. 18, (DJD II 101), and compare to the Greek bill Mur. 114, for the parallel word. For the procedural and not contractual significance of this verb : Seidl, PtRG 61; H.J. Wolff, ZSS Rom. Abt. LXXIV (1957) 54.

[6] Compare the expression *admissions and loans* (TB Sanhedrin 2b), apparently denoting the two modes of testimony of a debt, and M Sanhedrin III 6.

no more than a *bill of admission*. Just as in former times the witnesses
would testify to the act of acquisition of title done by the purchaser
with the agreement or acquiescence of the seller (Ruth IV 8-10), so
also a bill granting title and a bill of divorcement testify to words of
the grantor. But in so doing they eventually make the act *constitutive*
(M Qiddushin I 1-3, 5). Admissions took on a set formula according to
which the admitting party verified the fact, and this formula took the
place of the act of acquisition which preceded the writing of the documents (Ruth IV 7). In some cases the party signs *on himself*, i.e.
as a promisor and not as a witness;[1] in other he declares before the
witnesses that the contents of the bill is *true*, in one of the expressions
firm and true (TB Baba Bathra 160b), *true firm and clear* (TJ Gittin
IX 9.50c), "I A the son of B undertake what is written in this bill"
(T Baba Meṣia I 13), "I A have borrowed from B" (T Baba Bathra
XI 4).[2]

Verification of the bill was in these cases done by the promisor in
the presence of the witnesses. However, it could also be done by the
witnesses—before a court. Therefore if a bill is produced in a suit it
is challenged—"it shall be *verified* by its signers" (M Gittin I 3).[3] The
court would summon the witnesses by whom the bill was signed in
order that they *verify* their own signatures.[4]

A similar procedure was used in other cases : "Where a man's promissory note has been obliterated the witnesses testify to it and he
comes before a court and they make him a *verification* : "A the son
of B—his bill was obliterated on day C, and D and E are its witnesses"
(M Baba Bathra X 6).[5]

Following rules of halakha that deal with unusual cases, the meaning
of *verification* became extended so far as to become synonymous with
the *constitutive* effect of the bill. It is this that was meant by the saying
that the husband should not write his wife's bill of divorcement, since

---

[1] Thus in the Elephantine bills, E. Volterra, Mélanges E. Tisserant, Roma 1964, I,
443-448, and also in the Murabbaat bills and in the Talmud.

[2] Such a formula is found already in the Elephantine bills, Yaron, in Bibliotheca
orientalis XV (1958) 20 ff. and compare the expression *true and firm* in confirmation
of recitation of the *Shema* (TB Berakhoth 12a). Regarding the formula see M. Hässler,
Die Bedeutung der Kyria-Klausel in den Papyrusurkunden, Berlin 1960; Gulak Urkundenwesen, 26 ff. As to the declaration before witnesses or in public : F. Pringsheim,
The Greek Law of Sale, Weimar 1950, 18 ff.

[3] This clause continues clause 1, and precedes the view of Rabban Gamliel.

[4] Cf. the procedure of confirmation described in TB Kethuboth 21a.

[5] See T Baba Bathra XI 8-9.

"a bill of divorcement can only be *verified* by its signers" (M Gittin II 5).

Important bills would be deposited in the *archeia* in the Temple;[1] in this *archeia* there were special witnesses for verifying the bill and for notarial functions (M Qiddushin IV 5). Even if it was not deposited in the *archeia*, the bill could be delivered to the custody of a court (M Shebi'ith X 2),[2] and then a court messenger would effect collection. It was also possible to deposit the bill with a third party, so that the debtor could not claim that it had been forged or unlawfully altered (T Baba Meṣia I 13).

Depositing with the *archeia* was customary as well in regard to bills granting title, especially if the grant was made by way of a will : "If he wrote and sent it up to the *archeia*, the *archeia* acquired title for their benefit" (T Baba Bathra VIII 2-3) : even though the bill was not delivered to the purchaser, it received effect by virtue of being deposited in the *archeia*.

A bill was generally written in relation to a debt due on a loan or some other cause. However, a bill of *admission* could of itself create the debt : "If he wrote in favour of a priest that he owes him five *selas*—he must give him" (M Bekhoroth VIII 8, TB Kethuboth 101b). This is also the *ratio* of the doctrine whereby after-acquired property may be charged : the charge can only be valid by virtue of *admission* : "Payment from property which I have and which I may henceforth acquire" (TJ Kethuboth IV 8. 29a ; T Kethuboth IV 12).[3]

Thus we find that bills granting title and bills of emancipation were originally no more that *evidentiary* bills, and later on became *constitutive* documents. Therefore these bills were couched in terms of *admission*" 'I have made A my slave a freeman', 'he is made a

---

[1] Josephus, II War XVII 6.427. Regarding the Hellenistic practice of depositing bills see : F. v. Woess, Untersuchungen über das Urkundenwesen und den Publizitäts-schutz im römischen Aegypten (MB,6), München 1924; Bickerman, Institutions, 209; Seidl PtRG, 62 ff.

[2] A person merely delivering his bills does not write a *prosbol*, as the Mishna distinguishes between the two. This distinction was drawn also by Maimonides and the Tosafists. *Rashi*, on the other hand, perhaps following Sifre Deut. 113, considers the two identical.

[3] Such a charge appears in Demotic bills in Egypt from the fourth century B.C.E. onward; so also in Murabbaat 18.30 and in the Greek bills Dura Europos 22 and Mur. 114. Cf. Liebermann, Tos. Kif. Kethuboth IV 12; Gulak, Urkundenwesen, 55 f., 116. As I have attempted to show, the bill of admission is of greater antiquity than reference to the Sages of the Talmud at TB Baba Bathra 149a.

freeman', 'behold he is a freeman', 'I have given X', 'it is given to X', 'behold it is his' (TB Gittin 40b).[1] All these expressions are *admissions*, by virtue of which title was vested. Similarly, bills of sale included an *admission* on the part of the seller that he received his money and that he effected the transaction of his own will.[2]

In some cases we find in bills granting title an *admission* of the grantor's wife that she *waives* the subjection of the property to her rights under her marriage contract. She may say "I have no right or claim against you" (M Kethuboth X 6), or she may furnish her own *responsibility* to the purchaser (T Gittin V (III) 2), in other words—to add to her husband's bill of sale : and I X his wife am *responsible*.[3]

The first bill granting title was apparently one of gift. Whereas in sale the property is transferred by payment of money, and the bill is merely *evidentiary*, in gift it is the bill itself that *gives title*. Hence the term *gift* came ro denote not only the transaction but also the bill testifying to it.[4]

However there remain in the bill of sale traces of oral granting of title, from the time that the bill was merely *evidentiary*. The giver generally says that he *vested* the recipient (T Baba Bathra VIII 9),[5] and such *vesting* is an act of acquisition by a garment, performed by the witnesses in favour of the recipient. Thus even though "liable property may be acquired ... *by bill*" (M Qiddushin I 5), the ancient *attestation* (Ruth IV 8) was still retained in practice.[6]

It is mainly in wills that the application appeared of the oral transaction and the bill accompanying it. The father could command his sons as to what should be done after his death, and this command would be oral. Thus, Aqabya b. Mahalalel's son said to him "*commend me to your colleagues*" (M Eduyoth V 7), and heirs could argue that they could swear "that Father did not *command* us and Father did

---

[1] The version according to the Munich MS.

[2] In the Elephantine bills the expression is *the goodness of my heart :* on this see Y. Muffs, Studies in Aramaic Legal Papyri from Elephantine, (Studia et Documenta, 8), Leiden 1968. In the bills of Judean Desert the seller declares that he received the money and that he did the act of his own will Murr. 24, and cf. E. Koffmahn, Die Doppelurkunden aus der Wüste Juda, Leiden 1968, 66.

[3] Cf. Mur. 26, in which the wife makes herself responsible.

[4] There is a similarity to this in Greek law : see Kunkel, RE *syngraphe*. And as to the bill granting title in Hellenistic Egypt : Cl. Préaux, Recueil Société Jean Bodin VI (1965) 194-205.

[5] See also T Gittin I 8.

[6] Cf. the same duplicity in biblical times : Iura XIX (1968) 113 ff.

not say to us" (M Shebu'oth VII 7). Later on, however, it became the custom to write a *bill of command* (TB Gittin 50 b), which served both as evidence and as grant of title.[1]

---

[1] See JJS XII (1961) 67 ff. This may be the place to mention the custom of expressing the finality of the transaction in bills of gift. In the Elephantine bills the donor declares that the matter shall have effect "in my life and at my death" (Kraeling, AP 10; Cowley, AP 8), and in M Baba Bathra VIII 7 : "from today and after death". This form is designed not only to transfer the property immediately and the income after death (see R. Yaron, Gift in Contemplation of Death, Oxford 1960, 114 ff.), but also to prevent the donor from retracting. In this respect the formula is this of "a gift from today until the time that I wish" (T Kethuboth IX 2).